# CONCILIUM
*Theology in the Age of Renewal*

# CONCILIUM

*Theology in the Age of Renewal*

Volume 59: Spirituality

# DIMENSIONS
# OF SPIRITUALITY

Edited by
Christian Duquoc

Herder and Herder

1970
HERDER AND HERDER
232 Madison Avenue, New York 10016

*Cum approbatione Ecclesiastica*

Library of Congress Catalog Card Number: 78–129758

Printed in the United States

# CONTENTS

PART III

# DOCUMENTATION CONCILIUM

# Editorial

CHRISTIAN theology is at last beginning to remind itself that the biblical writers were witnesses to a promise. God's future inhabited their present. Today, the future haunts us and a man like Ernst Bloch has built up a philosophy centred on hope. Bloch takes his inspiration from Marx. However, our awareness of the future is ambivalent. There is a shift taking place in contemporary attitudes. Following on the period at the end of the last century in which man idolized progress, we are seeing the beginnings of a more suspecting era. Scientific and technological discoveries no longer produce naïve confidence in their power to change life. Industrial organization, the product of technology and science, is often accused of being "repressive": it leaves us no room for freedom and happiness. Far from being controlled by science and technology, conflicts are exacerbated and our increased power renders them infinitely more harmful to the human race than before. Expectations have met with disappointment: writers from the East do not offer reassurance as to the human consequences of the Marxist-inspired political systems. The enchanted future causes crimes in the present. Western societies, too, are torn with contradictions: ill-distributed abundance gives rise to revolt, and frequently boredom and despair.

Christians are not exempt from the ambivalence of the future in our time. They are losing confidence in their Churches. The introduction of socio-political methods into the analysis of Church institutions too frequently reveals them to be regressive factors and obstacles to freedom. They appear to have only limited

7

scope for development. The effectiveness of the witness they bear and their practical strength seem to be very largely illusory. If life must change, many believers think that this change will come about in spite of or in opposition to the Churches.

These considerations underlie our choice of the subject of hope for this issue of *Concilium* devoted to *Spirituality*. The first article describes the current crisis and how it affects Christian hope. Jesus is not only the object or the support of this hope but also its witness. His historical life did not escape the ambivalence which the future has for us. This is the theme of the second article. Why this ambivalence portraying contradictory attitudes? Is hope based on reason or illusion? Why do utopias keep springing up? Has despair a place in the heart of our Christian faith? These are the themes of the third, fourth and fifth articles.

The bulletins are devoted to the same topic, with more emphasis on supplying facts: an account of the philosophy of Ernst Bloch, brief bibliographical notes on the German theology of hope. Others point out the radical implications of the messianic songs of American Negroes and the fascination of Asian religions.

In an age in which many people are filled with despair, the important thing is not to offer consolation or entertain a false optimism, but to remind ourselves that the biblical promise did not exempt those who bear witness to it from the long dark night of waiting. God's Word does not enable us to calculate the chances of a happy future. But it is present in all our attempts to ward off fate.

CHRISTIAN DUQUOC
CLAUDE GEFFRÉ

# PART I
## ARTICLES

Karl Gastgeber

# The Contemporary Crisis and the Birth of New Models of Hope

## Preliminary Remarks

THE first question is whether there is any profound crisis in the way that the problems of economics, politics, sociology and intellectual and religious life are shaping throughout the world, or whether these are simply normal phenomena of growth and change that have existed at all times. Life cannot continue without tension between tradition and progress, continuity and adaptation. Compared with the high percentage of conservative groups in the population of every country, radical revolutions appear as exceptions or isolated events. Strongly progressive periods in history are always followed by periods of markedly conservative tendency.

It is, however, possible to speak of a world-wide crisis today, the causes of which should be investigated, in so far as they are susceptible of a rational analysis and do not remain hidden in the inscrutable, irrational ground of temporal events, part of those forces of destiny that lie within the providence of God and withheld from human understanding.

## I. The Causes of the Present Crisis

It is impossible to give a comprehensive account of the crisis or its causes, given the complex flux of events in our present-day world. We can only hope to outline a few aspects of it.

A typical crisis of growth has come about through the structural change from an agrarian to an industrial society—probably the greatest of its kind in the history of mankind. In 1850 80% of our population was involved in primary agriculture, and 10% each in secondary industry and service. In 1950 50% was working in secondary industry and 25% each in the primary and tertiary areas. By the year 2000 the distribution of occupations will be practically reversed: primary industry will account for 5% at the most, with 10% in secondary and 85% in tertiary industry. This will involve far-reaching changes in family life, in the process of production and the spheres of human and political relations—changes which, even now, are emerging, amid much tension. Thus monarchy and patriarchalism have been superseded by democracy and collaboration, which are more appropriate to the social structures of today.

Socialism, intensified by the great rise in population, is a threat to the individual, but the individual is no longer able to fulfil those obligations once carried out by the family (such as the care of the sick and the aged). It is increasingly necessary for social institutions to assume responsibility for people's general welfare. The superstructures of the secondary powers (*sekundären Mächte*), the establishment and social apparatus of the State are becoming man's second nature. He who rebels against it perishes. It is here that we see most clearly the loss of a man's individuality in the mass. The democratization of the whole of social life has been only the necessary further stage towards that total system of human manipulation that is today regarded as a threat to man's freedom. Moreover, pluralist systems induce insecurity and force men continually to make important decisions. Society seeks to influence everyone through manipulation, whether in favour of an ideology or a political system. The mind of the masses can be altered by scientific, technical and psychological means—propaganda, advertising, indoctrination and brain-washing. Their effect is heightened by the mass media and creates insecurity and anxiety in the population. Reducing all things to the rational and the scientific alienates man, who then seeks to protect himself through an unemotional and objective attitude to life.

The basis of the consumer society is the steadily increasing use of goods, and there is a whole army of hidden persuaders to seduce man into an ever higher degree of consumption. He is persuaded that his standard of living, his clothes, car, housing, etc., are what determine his status in society. Leisure time, longed for by the individual, is not now used by him in his own way, but is managed by impersonal bodies. Man today is not threatened by sickness, plague, wars and famine so much as by the self-manipulation of society, where one small error in the machinery can destroy his whole existence. Modern city life and the swiftly expanding sciences impose a mental burden on him that he is unable to support. He is continually forced to make important decisions involving rational and abstract thought, decisions for which he lacks the necessary information, knowledge or moral maturity. This can produce anxiety and an inferiority complex. Fearing his own decisions, man flees to mass ideologies.

Let us now pinpoint a few specific elements of crisis within the social system of the West which exemplify this general endangering of human life. The first thing that we notice is the tremendous decline in the confidence in, and credibility of, the traditional order and attitudes. This is shown in the outbreaks of violence and brutality, culminating in extreme terrorist activities (the race riots in the U.S.A., the religious riots in Northern Ireland, and the student riots in Paris). According to the depth psychologists, these aggressive and criminal acts are generally the product of anxieties and disappointed hopes, and hence nothing but a desperate cry for help. Another terrifying fact is the increase in crime: in the U.S.A., for example, as high as 11% last year, with cases of robbery with violence as high as 18% more than in the previous year. Every hour there are fifty cases of murder and manslaughter.

A further symptom of social disintegration is the sharp rise in drug-taking. According to reliable reports, between 20% and 35% of American students are addicted to hashish and other drugs. It may be true that the use of drugs is the expression of protest against the existing social structure, with the hippie movement chiefly responsible for the popularization of hashish, LSD and other drugs, in its attempt to win youth away from traditional values and the ambitious striving for success. It must still, however, be regarded as the expression of doubt in the meaning of life and a profound hopelessness as regards the future. H. Marcuse's criticism of the repressive society of today underlies

the non-violent hippie movement, which seeks to impose a new
way of life on society with its slogan "Make love, not war".

Herbert Marcuse has abandoned his earlier Marxist optimism.
He sees existing society as an inhuman system of exploitation
and oppression to which even the workers have succumbed. In
an age of advanced industrialization men have been largely reduced to a common mental denominator, they no longer have
any independence or dynamic hope for the future. The manipulation of the mind in the age of technology and science is complete. The whole of human life is becoming one-dimensional, and
it is impossible to break out of it. From this situation Marcuse
draws radical conclusions. Criticism must be directed in the most
radical way against the dominant reality principle and not be
afraid of even the absurd and the vulgar. A social system based
on productivity leads inevitably to rivalry and war among peoples.
He sees the salvation of man in a society in which man is not enslaved by institutions which alienate man from himself and
whose repressive effects prevent him from discovering his real
self. He derives his social anthropology from Marx and Freud,
with the difference that he rejects the sublimation of the instincts.
For him the goal is to bring about, by artistic and orphic means,
the liberation of man from all repression. The salvation of the
future ages of mankind lies only in his emancipation from the
profit motive, the influence of forces that alienate him from himself, as well as from the destructive power of his own selfishness.
We can see here parallels with St Augustine's idea of the *Civitas
Dei*, in which slavery and manipulation are overcome by greater
freedom and the desire for peace. And the short circuit of existential selfishness is wholly lacking.

This world-wide criticism of our society and the desire for
reform is not limited solely to followers of Marcuse and the hippie
movement, but has produced its own forms of contestation in
the spheres of ideology, politics and the Church. Public opinion
is moving away from conservatism, and traditional society now
finds its supporters only among a few radical right-wing groups.
Pragmatic and programmatic reforms are drawn up by scientists
and responsible politicians and officials. Within the Church a
more radical attitude is taken by those reformers who have moved
beyond Roman canon law, scholasticism and the neo-Thomist

conception of natural law and are seeking a new path for the people of God that is more in accordance with modern insights into anthropology by continual reference back to the Bible and the post-apostolic tradition. The revolutionary reformers are seeking to overthrow the constitution and the law. They stand outside the legal order and believe that only in this way are they able to overcome oppression. In the Church they call for a radical change in the way the Church looks at itself, for the setting up of advisory councils (*Rätesystems*), the end of obedience and celibacy, and the substitution of a political goal for the Church's religious one.

Those who favour this kind of radical contestation are to be found in politically and ideologically orientated youth organizations, especially at universities. The background to this is the break-up of values and beliefs, as well as the difficult situation (*Selbstfindung*) of the primary groups and the speed at which change takes place. Young people have adopted a syncretist, neo-Marxist, neo-Freudian social ideology, as a result of the over-cultivation of formal intelligence at the expense of a meaningful knowledge of the object. Also, the formative forces have moved from the inner to the outer sphere: the family is losing its influence, whereas the bewilderingly complex outside world has too little capacity to shape a person. There is a notably high percentage of young people who are psychologically at risk. They are led by a false ethos of freedom to plan a new social order that bears no continuity with the old and is lacking in any social compulsion. They come to grief when they collide with reality, whose structures and traditions prove more resilient and longer-lived than the technical processes which people are afraid will enslave them to technocracy. By a mental short circuit all institutions are totally rejected and their representatives denied all authority. The social structures of other peoples which are still evolving are taken over holus bolus (viz., the cults of Che Guevara, Mao and Ho Chi Minh) and applied to our own capitalist society. This impedes the sound investigation of those conditions in our own society that need reform.

If society is to be preserved, the measures to be taken today by society and the Church in regard to the protest movement are as follows:

(1) The renunciation of force in the carrying out of reforms;
(2) an objective and comprehensive plan for the future;
(3) a revaluation of the society that refuses to "hallow" any social conditions.

It would be fatal for both Church and society if they ignored the critical opposition groups within themselves or rejected them as irrelevant. The intellectual opposition would not forgive the Church if it came to regard "Catholic" and "intellectual" as irreconcilable opposites. These opposition movements may well contain some of that non-conformism enjoined by the Gospel, and of which St Paul speaks when he tells us not to liken ourselves to the world. This is an indication of the inner strength of these groups.

## II. THE ATTRACTION AND DYNAMICS OF THE FUTURE

Man's domination of nature has achieved results that have surpassed his wildest expectations. Technology and industry aim at doubling the social product within the foreseeable future. Then man would finally be able to banish poverty and suffering from the world. Automation reduces man's burden of labour, so that he can devote himself more to his cultural and social needs. The major part of the production potential will be available for art and science. A cultured and leisured society on an enormous scale is in store for us. The new social forms and institutions possess a strong dynamic, and the horizontal and vertical mobility of mankind has greatly increased. Already many millions of human beings are physically on the move, whether professionally or as tourists. The fact that mankind is growing more and more unified means that projects and industrial undertakings of all kinds are more interlinked, which involves greater mutual dependence and influence. The mushroom development of world trade is being increased through technology, modern transport, supermarkets and the mass media. The fate of mankind everywhere affects every individual human being; economic crises and wars have consequences that are world-wide. The unity of human history is clear to everyone, even in the remotest village. Moreover, peoples and nations are becoming more and more homogeneous.

A further dynamic factor is to be found in the increasing urbanization and the associated emergence of cultural peaks (*Hochkulturen*). The mass media make possible not only a total propagandistic domination of man's psyche, but also the extensive further development of society in terms of greater and greater achievements. As a result of differentiation and the division of labour we have a pluralist society in which the individual often has to play the most varied roles.

## III. THE LOSS OF RELIGIOUS SIGNIFICANCE

The autonomy of secular realities, proclaimed in the Pastoral Constitution (n. 36), accepts the logical conclusions of the process of secularization that is already familiar to us. Progress is outstripping faith. Demythologization and desacralization are only the first stages of a total secularization of the world. For the hominized world that man has shaped misses too often the transcendental realities, since they never appear in the immanent sphere. It is still an open question how far the influence of Teilhard de Chardin has opened up the way to the totality of the reality of the world within science as well, in an "extended physics" and "humanity" of the sciences. The most exciting and most dangerous discoveries today are undoubtedly in the fields of biophysics and genetics; their aim is to bring about profound changes in human society.

## IV. SECULARIZATION

It is a mark of their independence that science, culture and art no longer regard themselves as tied to sacred "traditions" but consider as true only what they themselves are able to verify and realize. Society itself is no longer created "by the grace of God", but by the people. A religious interpretation of reality is rejected as unnecessary. Thus the Church itself is drawn today into a process of secularization. It is now able to see itself as only one element in society, competing with various other ideologies and views of the world. It no longer has the monopoly in upholding a scale of values and public morality. Of course it does have the advantage of a longer tradition and superior experience,

2—C.

but its prestige is dwindling, since the values of the Church have apparently become meaningless in terms of day-to-day living.

## V. New Models of Hope

### (a) *Human and Philosophical Systems*

The most important contribution that has been made in this area is Ernst Bloch's "Hope Principle". For Ernst Bloch religion is hope, and hope is grounded in this ontic difference between what exists and what does not yet exist, between *Vorhandenheit* and *Zukünftigkeit*, both in man and in the cosmos. Man as an entity whose being is not yet fully fashioned is himself "a task to be worked at as well as his environment, and a great container of the future". Part of hope is the knowledge that life outside is just as unfinished a thing as the ego that is helping to fashion it. Thus religion, inasmuch as it offers hope, is grounded in the process character of man and the world.

"God", for Bloch, is the *"homo absconditus"* of the future, as yet unfound and unachieved. Thus God, as the image and reflection of man, is reduced, not to the sensuous presence of man, not to the alienated, antagonistic social (p. 316) situation of man, but to the "unfound" future *humanum"*. "God" is the utopian hypostasized ideal of the unknown man" (Jürgen Moltmann, *Theologie der Hoffnung*, Munich 1966, pp. 316/7).

If, then, hope is so world-immanent, if in our perfect age, in which we see to the bottom of things, God is no longer necessary, then the ideal of perfection will naturally be projected on to the social life of man, on to peace and justice, an ideal world and the highest possible development of the individual. Thus we find, for example, that the inhibitions of traditional sex education fall away and indulgence is regarded as more appropriate to the nature of man. Ernst Bloch has defined his "hope principle" as living, not on the basis of "an empirically developed *adaequatio intellectus ad rem*, but of a creative *inadaequatio* of the understanding in regard to the practical"; in other words, living not on the basis of truth, but of active hope.

The criticism is made of him that he places the focus of the "creative *adaequatio* of the reason in regard to the practical" within the potentiality of contemporary man. If, then, the utopian norm lies within man himself, then the future is measured against something static, against what man, what we today, regard as right; so that objectivist truth would still triumph over dynamic hope. When society takes from man his economic, social and political worries, and general production begins to be regulated "automatically", Marx's "realm of freedom" will have come about; but then Bloch sees as "more pressing than ever the real worries, the question of what really does not add up about life".

Against a society incurably marred by manipulation and domination, H. Marcuse sets another quite new and different one: this is characterized by freedom from the institution, which he sees as the structure of alienated domination of the will. Man's real nature is to be realized. Marcuse's hypothesis of a non-repressive culture is bound up with the non-suppression of drives, a non-repressive development of the libido. He attempts to fuse the social theory of Marx and the psychoanalysis of Freud.

### (b) *Models of Christian Hope*

J. Moltmann's criticism of Ernst Bloch is that his "hope principle" threatens to disintegrate. One of two things will happen. Either infinite hope will transcend all the finite objects of hope that it sets before itself. Then hope becomes the eternal, unhistorical existential of man, and the life process of the world becomes an endless process. But this would be an abstraction from real history. Being-in-hope would become the abstract definition of man. Or else transcendent hope will eventually become assimilated to a utopian object of hope and be satisfied, as, for example, by "socialist achievements". But then it betrays itself. Thus all utopias of the kingdom of God or man, all images of hope of the happy life, all revolutions of the future remain in the air and bear within themselves the seed of decay and boredom and therefore have an aggressive and blackmailing attitude towards life, for as long as there is no certainty in death and no hope that would carry love beyond death. According to Bultmann's existential theology every moment can have an eschatological quality and reveal the ultimate meaning of history. "The timeless becomes an event, the non-worldly comes into the world, the logos becomes flesh—this is the mystery of New Testament eschatology" (*Kerygma und Mythos*, vol. 1, Hamburg, 1948, p. 146).

But this eschatology of the present proves to be self-deception when confronted by the ontological forces of time, which is constantly passing away into nothing, and by all-destroying death.

F. Kerstiens points out that the revelation of God was given to us as a promise. The centre of revelation is Jesus Christ himself. In the cross and resurrection of Jesus the limits of this world are transcended and a universal horizon of salvation opened up. God does not impart some truth, but *himself* as the salvation and the future of man and his world. Hence hope is a mode of faith and thus a power to withstand the darkness of fate. Hope hopes for the one future of all natural and supernatural orders. It also preserves the Church from narrowness and makes dialogue with unbelievers possible. Hope is a *"docta spes"*, since its basis is the promises of God and the memory of his faithful love, shown in the history of his people, and especially in the cross and resurrection of his Son. Hope is not the enemy of tradition, but precisely the power of its orientation towards a final fulfilment. . . . Hope is directed towards the new creation of the world by God and the salvation of all men in the new world. Hence it overcomes individualism and pure personalism, on the one hand, and collectivism on the other. Hope, ultimately, is trust in the saving will of God for all men and faith in the cross of Christ as a sign of the redemption of mankind. (F. Kerstiens, *Hoffnungsstruktur des Glaubens*, Mainz, 1969, p. 228.)

*Translated by William Glen-Doepel*

# Christian Duquoc

# The Hope of Jesus

MANY people today claim Jesus Christ as the approver of their ideas, their struggles or their passions. They project on to him characteristics necessary to a leader who arouses or stimulates the masses. The titles that the New Testament attributed to Jesus appear obsolete: they prefer names that are more committed or more emotional. He is in turn the pal, the comrade, the revolutionary, the "che". It would be wrong to underestimate these nominations which are either spontaneous or the outcome of political fashion. They are evidence of a significant claim: the hero, leader or model can only carry out his function by belonging flesh and blood to the group or community that he unites. Jesus opened a way, and this way appears today to many to assume first of all a political significance. The praying Christ hardly attracts; the hieratic Christ of St John's gospel seems a stranger; the risen Lord of the kerygmatic preaching, the Son of God of Paul's epistles, the Saviour and the High Priest of the Epistle to the Hebrews are remote and are for many without practical significance. There remains the historical conflict of Jesus against the authorities. This conflict is close to our own conflicts. Jesus, the man, the prophetic preacher and yet one of us, becomes the fountain-head of political contestation or the guarantor of revolutionary mystique.

This new perception of Jesus comes more directly from living than from theoretical structure. It calls for a critical evaluation that the theologies of the Revolution in their spontaneous generosity feel reluctant to undertake. In the present article, I have no intention of validating or invalidating this way of seeing things. I take it as a symptom of very positive intuitions. I see in it an invitation to take the historical struggle of Jesus seriously.

To traditional thought, caricatured here, that is to say transmitted as well as received without criticism and without variation, the historical Jesus is the obedient executor of a pre-established plan: he fulfils the will of the Father, say the gospels. The Christian who is not attentive to the language of the Scriptures or not sufficiently spiritual imagines simply that this will was a plain imperative for Jesus. His death is included in this plan, it arises from a mysterious necessity, it is true, but its significance is not contested. Obscurity is on our side. All our efforts should tend towards assimilating, submissively, the clear understanding that Jesus had of God's plan.

This way of understanding God's plan for Jesus does not satisfy: is the death of Jesus a human death if he knows that "the stakes are already down"? Jesus in that case felt neither our hesitations nor our anguish. He would have followed a way that was clearly marked out. His obedience, evidence of his confidence in the Father, imprints on the necessity of his death, brought about by the sins of men and their limited mentality, a voluntary character which would deprive it of the horror of an outside phenomenon from which there is no escape: "Therefore doth my Father love me," says the Christ of St John, "because I lay down my life, that I might take it again. No man taketh it from me, but I lay it down of myself. I have power to lay it down, and I have power to take it again" (John 10. 17–18). Through this freedom, Jesus would therefore already have overcome death. The future is for him an open book. The risk is averted: neither the extinction of his liberty nor the conspiracy of sordid interests will interfere with the success of his task. Human history is finally tamed. But how can we speak of the hope of a man who has conquered the world? "The history of the world would certainly be very easy to shape if the conflict were only undertaken when one could count on infallible chances of success."[1]

The traditional thought that I have reduced to bare outline

[1] K. Marx, *Werke*, ed. *MEGA* (Berlin), vol. xxxiii, p. 209.

purposely to show how scandalous it is to a modern mind does not allow for the inclusion of any feeling similar to that of hope in the historical development of Jesus. Consequently, does the experience of Jesus affect us if it is true that we could not have a clear idea of the will of God? Are the terms attributed by certain Christians to Jesus, which presuppose the fact of a struggle and of a human fraternity, anything else but the projection of our desires? Is it true that the transcendent qualities recognized by the primitive Church in Jesus actually wrest him from our obscure situation where good and evil are neither sure nor absolute? Would Jesus, as risen Lord, just be the support or upholder of our hope? Must he be denied all experience of what appears so radical in our relations with the future, with hope? Or should we not rather concede to the new perceptions of Jesus in the depths of his humanity the intuition of a fundamental fact of his historical existence forgotten by the classical theologians? This way seems more productive: Jesus is not only the objective prop to our hope through his resurrection, he is also the one who first actively showed hope in the darkness of our history. If he is a "model", perhaps it is not so much through his transcendent titles as through the human quality in which they took root. The conditions in which he exercised hope were comparatively the same as ours.

In an exploration of the hope of Jesus it would be wrong to allow oneself to be impressed by the lack of direct evidence in the New Testament. Thus the items "hope" in the different biblical dictionaries are silent on the attitude of Jesus: either they point out the eschatological content of the preaching of Jesus, his expectation of the Kingdom of God, or else they give as the object and foundation of Christian hope the risen Christ. The hope of Jesus in his historical development is not mentioned.[2]

To be sure, the gospels are not biographies. Yet they do not leave us without some indication of the attitude of Jesus: as proof I give the scene of derision at the foot of the cross. It is related

[2] This is true of the dictionaries I have consulted: *Theologisches Wörterbuch z.N.T.*, Band II, art. "Elpis" by R. Bultmann, pp. 525 ff. X. L. Dufour, *Vocabulaire de Théologie Biblique*, art. "Espérance" (Paris, 1964), columns 305–310. Von Allmen, *Vocabulaire biblique*, Delacheaux, art. "Espérance".

by the three Synoptics in forms which are relatively close (Matthew 27. 42–44; Mark 15. 32–33; Luke 23. 35): "He saved others," say the High Priests and Pharisees, "himself he cannot save." This impotence of Jesus in regard to himself is contradictory to the power he displays in favour of others, think the rulers. This difference of power in respect of himself and of others denounces Jesus as an impostor, according to them, and confirms the malediction of God. The titles usurped by him prove the falsehood: he had called himself King of Israel and Son of God, according to Matthew's version; Messiah and King of Israel according to Mark; the Anointed One of God, the Chosen One, according to Luke. All these titles with which Jesus would have tried to define his identity accuse him. Thus condemned, he is going to die. If he breaks the destiny weighing upon him, we shall see, say the mockers according to Mark. Then will be the time to believe. The Chief Priests and Scribes require from Jesus a demonstration of power in favour of himself. If he has demonstrated this power in respect of others, what obstinacy or deception restrains him from action? Let him attend to himself, that is let him save his own life and his preaching will acquire credibility. Matthew sheds light on this scene with a quotation borrowed from Psalm 22 verse 9: "he trusted in God, let God deliver him seeing he delighted in him". God's neglect of him proclaims the judgment of condemnation. Jesus is accused: his claim to be a friend of God was only a falsehood. Jesus himself as he is dying quotes the first verse of this psalm: "My God, my God, why hast thou forsaken me?"

This scene of insults and this cry of Jesus are an opening to the understanding of his hope. For the Scribes and Pharisees, as for the mockers in Psalm 22, the death of the one who claims to be just shouts out the falsity of his justness. This scene summarizes and symbolizes the situation in which Jesus performed an act of hope in God.

The preaching by Jesus of the coming of the Kingdom of God cannot be separated from the attitude which was his. According to Bultmann, the life of Jesus was not "messianic". This thesis, often badly understood, underlines the scandalous nature of his historical life if it is judged according to the criteria of traditional messianism. It makes certain fundamental ideas in the gospels

more coherent: the messianic secret in Mark, the literary structure of the temptations, the accounts of the agony and death. It
gives an indirect opening to the understanding of the subjective
hope of Jesus.

Jesus' recommendation in Mark, to say nothing of his messianity (he silences the devils and orders the apostles not to tell
of the glory of his transfiguration), is an editorial device which
implies that his messianity is only perceptible when one starts
from faith in his resurrection. This does not mean that the
people did not recognize him as the Messiah and that his messianity lacked manifestations: the accounts of his trial imply the
contrary. But these signs have never formed a picture of messianic behaviour which conforms to the pre-established image.
This misapprehension explains how they could call him an impostor with a minimum of probability. An analysis of the accounts of the temptations, the agony and the death would lead
to similar remarks. The messianity required a demonstration of
the power of God in favour of his people. His representative
was the mediator of this power. None of this occurred. Jesus
cannot be the one who is awaited. Apparently, Jesus finds himself in the situation of the righteous man whose prayer is given in
Psalm 22: he is subjected to mockery for everything predicts that
God does not care about him. Jesus, Messiah and Son of God
that he was, did not benefit from a situation which was privileged in comparison with that of the righteous men of the Old
Testament. He hopes that God will fulfil his promises, but this
hope is apparently without foundation and without verification.
The traditional Messiah must, on the contrary, verify by wield-
ing the power of God in the face of the enemies of his people
that the promise had not been an empty one. It is the hope of
the people, the demonstration of the power of God by the breaking of his too lengthy silence which is the temptation of Jesus.
Jesus comes up against a stronger inconsistency than that of the
righteous men of the Old Testament: they were awaiting the
realization of the promise. Jesus announces the imminent irruption of the Kingdom.

The Kingdom is coming but Jesus does not hasten the time.
He hopes sufficiently in God not to force destiny: changing stones
into bread, enticing through miracles, forcing happiness on the

crowds by exercising political power would to all appearances have been the methods of a Messiah. The source of the revolution or the transformation of society would have been supernatural. It would not because of this have ceased to be earthly. For the sign of his messianism would have been power, and to understand power does not demand a "conversion" of the heart. Jesus is dedicated to the very feeblest of means. To "convince" he has only his attitude and his word. This extreme weakness, this renouncement of all the apparatus of power even to allowing himself to be accused of imposture, are the sign of the greatest hope in God: he accomplishes what he promises here where the authenticity of his countenance is revealed. God is not faithful to a plan, but to himself, that is to say, to the love he bears for men. To impose himself by power would not be manifesting his life; it would be adopting what the "world" in the Johannine sense instinctively worships. Jesus, Prophet and Revealer, assumes the risk of proclaiming the coming of the Kingdom in the feebleness of the Word. The risk was not imaginary: it was verified by his condemnation to death.

The death of Jesus was not "natural". He did not fade away, satiated with days as all pious Jews wished. It was the result of a trial, an inflicted death. The society of that time could not tolerate Jesus. Enemies as they were, Pharisees and Herodians became allies to remove this "prophet" whose liberty disturbed and whose word shook the common certainties. Jesus was declared a subversive and condemned as such.

The hope of Jesus explains this struggle against the established powers who assume the right to define the way of God. For him "the Spirit moves where it will, and no one knows from whence it comes, nor whither it goes". The Kingdom of God which he announces and for which he is hoping can be seen in his attitude: deliverance of self to God and serene audacity in the midst of opposition.

Deliverance of self to God: the freedom from care that the utterances of Jesus betray is surprising. "Consider the lilies of the field: how they grow; they toil not, neither do they spin" (Matthew 6. 28). "Take therefore no thought for the morrow: for the morrow shall take thought for the things of itself. Sufficient unto the day is the evil thereof" (Matthew 6. 34). Jesus is, however, neither a dreamer nor a complacent optimist. These words convey in paradoxical fashion how completely different the Kingdom of God is from all other concerns, and suggest how God is impassioned with man. The God of Jesus is the One he describes in the parable of the prodigal son. There is no account to settle, he rejoices with the son. This God is neither cunning nor domineering. The only right attitude towards him is absolute confidence.

The confidence of Jesus is not naïvety. He knows what is in man. The curses he utters against the Pharisees, the Scribes and the wealthy are evidence of his lucid passion for the Kingdom and of the obstacles that his founding of it must overcome. He knows the fate of the prophets: all were put to death. He is under no illusion about his fate. He pursues his path with no less audacity. Serene audacity, it is true. Patient audacity. He knows the stakes of his preaching. He measures the misery of his contemporaries. He evaluates the capacity of the means within his power. Miracles and wonders could change destiny. "Thou couldest have no power at all against me except it were given thee from above," he replies to Pilate who boasts of his office (John 19. 11). "Thinkest thou that I cannot now pray to my Father, and he shall presently give me more than twelve legions of angels," he says to Peter who is ready for violence (Matthew 26. 53).

To found the Kingdom by power would have been to hide the face of God and to contradict the very meaning of Revelation. To found it in weakness and freedom was to take the risk of not seeing it come into being. Jesus enters actively into this risk. One person to sow and another to reap. God is faithful and it is in the "now" of this fidelity that the promised Kingdom is coming.

The resistance to the messianic temptations reveals the quality and the meaning of the hope of Jesus. To yield to them would have been to sacrifice to the immediacy of the Kingdom: "abundance of goods", as a psalm describes it. Abundance is a consequence, not a starting-point. Morals and religions seem to defer the moment of satisfaction. The messianic temptations require it to be immediate. However, the difference between the attitude of Jesus and the one the temptation suggests is not temporal: the carrying forward of satisfaction to the end of time or immediate satisfaction. It is qualitative: the hope of Jesus is not an economy of means or a policy of the satisfaction of desires. The end itself is the difference between one attitude and the other and not only in time.

The messianic temptations, indeed, do not challenge first and foremost the delay of the Kingdom. They distort the nature of divine communication. Fascination with the immediate, eagerness for wealth, hunger for power expose the quality of desire: such an interpretation is bad. Only "transformed" desire can endure waiting, that is to say, master time and satisfaction. Only transformed desire interprets the silence of God outside the framework of indifference or blasphemy. The Beatitudes do not proclaim an economy of desire, they rearrange values. Happy is he who is now persecuted for righteousness' sake. In an unhappy situation he is already living the happiness promised by God. To Peter, who rejects the passion of the Messiah, Jesus retorts: "Get behind me, Satan, you do not understand the things of God." The death of the Messiah is not a regrettable accident in the course of events. It is, in a world of fascination for the immediate and for power, the place of Revelation. That "Christ must die" emphasizes a necessity of fact. The persecution of the rightous man is inherent in the development of our world. Jesus' hope does not rest on blind optimism. It is rooted in an experience: happiness is linked with something other than "the storing up of riches". In persecution, in poverty, the Kingdom is already there.

The ancient theologians expressed this experience by attributing to the earthly Christ the instant vision of God and consequently the beatification of his soul. Already at the appointed time, he had only to hope for the glorification of his body and of his Church.

Today we are more sensitive to the truth of Jesus' humanity, more attentive to the humbling of the Son of whom St Paul speaks in the Epistle to the Philippians; we can hardly imagine Jesus the man seeing the face of God revealed. Yet this clumsy way of describing the joy of Jesus sparks off true insight: the human consciousness of Jesus cannot be separated from his condition as the Son; it requires an experience, however incipient and progressive, of a reality unimaginable to our understanding: it is the fact of being he who is loved by God the Father that is the object of his happiness. "This is my beloved Son in whom I am well pleased." To see God is the consequence of the way our desire relates to him. St Paul, in the hymn to the Philippians, states precisely that Jesus did not relate to God "as if to a prey". His joy is to do the will of the One who sent him. The terms "duty" and "obedience" falsify the reality. It is a question of something infinitely more radical: only joy received and lived in the greatest innocence and the greatest love would evoke what we are referring to. The Kingdom is first of all this link between the Father and the Son Jesus. It is this communion which excludes all designs for power. It is the experience of Jesus in the darkness of God's silence. This experience is the foundation of what he hopes for: that God may be all in all men.

The "now" of transformed desire, the reality of the communion, change the quality of messianic riches. For the tempter the Kingdom is a demonstration of power; for Jesus, it is genuine communion. The first hopes to be satisfied: his desire is of a narcissistic order; the second hopes that the love of which God is the source will be the cornerstone of all constructions to come. The weakness of the means used by Jesus to found the Kingdom comes from the aim of Revelation itself. In spite of the failure of his word, in spite of the mockery of those who contradict him, he does not give way to the temptation to save himself: he did not come to be served. "If the grain of seed does not die, it does not bear fruit." To escape from the silence of God on the cross itself would have been to challenge the aims of his messianism, in short to deny the original content of his hope: "love is as strong as death" (Cant. 8. 6). The weakness of God to save the one he has sent is the strength of his love. Raised from the earth, according to John, Jesus will draw everyone to him. Incapable at present of justifying himself, his reputation lost, he knows what it will cost not to play the game of the world, the game of power. But he hopes this extreme love will reverse "desire" and that the weakness of the Messiah will become the strength for "transformation". Evil can only be conquered by an excess of good.

The optimism which followed the Second World War in the

Church and in the political groups has been succeeded by a great weariness. In the Church, the Council has not produced the fruits for which many were waiting. In the world, the violence and the crimes of the war are forgotten and we see the passion for destruction reappearing everywhere. Many people thought that the lack of impact of the Gospel in our world came essentially from the archaism of the Church. Some even would like to "bring the house down" as they say, so that at last the Gospel may appear in its purity. Nervous irritation takes hold and the very limited effectiveness of all the reforms increases the irritation. Some lose hope or become impatient. They flirt with violence, imagining what a revolution Jesus would accomplish if he returned. He would change life at last.

Jesus' hope never took the form of a dream, nor perhaps of a utopia. He experienced to the extremity the difficulty of "changing life". He refused to tell his disciples when the Kingdom will come, he did not mask the failure of his preaching, he wept over Jerusalem, he was angered by the pettiness of the Scribes and the blindness of the Pharisees, he felt the shortsightedness of his disciples. None of this led him to lose hope, for the Kingdom is where there exists neither self-assessment nor demonstrations of power but communion with God. The joy of God can be shared in the deepest disappointment. If Jesus' hope had been founded on an estimation of the evolution of societies, on an improvement in human relationships, it would only be optimism needing verification. It was never that and that is why he was able to risk everything so that eternal communion with God could be shared by men.

*Translated by Rita Barker*

Johann Hofmeier

# Hope—Instinct,
# Passion and Understanding

THE dream of a better life in the future is something that has preoccupied men in all periods of history. The theme has recently
been traced throughout the centuries by Ernst Bloch in his major
work, *Das Prinzip Hoffnung*. In this book, he has made the
human emotion of expectation, which he calls "hope", the object of profound philosophical investigation. He did not undertake this historical study simply because he was interested in the
ideas of utopia that have prevailed in the past, of course. His
main aim has been to provide a basis of understanding for the
movement forward into the future. He is, in fact, only one among
many philosophers and others who are deeply concerned with
the future. It is now generally accepted that man is an essentially
historical being who is open to the future, and the implications
of this view of man are being widely discussed at the present
time. The age of belief in the future of man has undoubtedly
dawned and man would seem to enjoy the prospect of being able
vastly to enlarge the scope of his consciousness in the future. The
more available the forces of nature become to man, however, the
more involved become the problems of their control and the more
need there is for planning. It is therefore particularly important to
assess this belief in the future critically. If we do not do this, there
is always a danger of losing the present in a constant pursuit of
a better future. It is necessary to put this impulse forward into
the future to the test and to ascertain how strong it is and how
much trust we can place in it. It goes without saying, of course,
that it is impossible for anyone accurately to predict the future.

On the other hand, however, no one would attempt to claim that this movement forward into the future has reached its goal—it is, after all, not so much the individual as the whole of life that is involved in a great process of becoming. This gives rise to the pressing question about the activating principle, the force that impels the whole of life forward. Does human hope originate here?

## I. Instinct and Human Hope

### 1. *Instinctive Behaviour among Men and Animals*

Medieval theologians had a remarkably certain knowledge of man's instinctive behaviour. They know that he did not always move towards a predetermined goal or carry out a rationally conceived plan, but that he frequently allowed himself to be impelled, as it were "from behind", by the strength of his natural impulses, propensities or instincts. Animals were given a special place within the scheme of living beings in so far as they strove infallibly towards their goal. Man, on the other hand, was not necessarily bound to act according to instinct. According to Thomas Aquinas, "man's sensitive forces" act "autonomously and instinctively, possessing a propensity of their own which is not dependent on, but may even contradict reason and which comes from his own nature. These forces are, however, accessible to reason, are ordered by it and must be subject to it if they are to be moral. In themselves, they are irrational and it is in his reason that man's greatness and dignity are, after all, to be found."[1]

Nothing that is essentially different from this is claimed by the idea of man based on biology, despite the fact that it has a narrower concept of instinct and man is given a special position among living beings. Apart from those spheres in which organs are active, there are, according to Arnold Gehlen, no genuinely instinctive actions in the case of man. Human behaviour is formed by an interaction with the world of other men, and man is distinguished by the fact that he is not bound by instincts. It is precisely because he is no longer determined by his instincts

[1] M. Seckler, *Instinkt und Glaubenswille nach Thomas von Aquin* (Mainz, 1961), p. 55.

that he is free and able to transform the conditions of his existence himself. There is in man a "completely unique but not yet fully tried out design".[2] The animal, on the other hand, has no future and moves, as it were, in a circle. What lies ahead of it is no more than the following segment of the circle. The animal is bound to act instinctively and, because of instinct, is blind to anything that is new and is chained, for better or for worse, to its environment.[3]

According to this view, then, impulsive or instinctive behaviour has no future. There can be no connection between being impelled "from behind" and moving rationally towards a goal. This may, of course, apply to the short period during which man lives and it may perhaps even apply to the whole period of human history that is accessible to scientific investigation. It certainly does not, however, apply to instinct as a whole, that is, the force that is inherent in all living beings and which helps them to develop further. Although it is true to say that no one can predict future evolution, this does not mean that there is no further evolution. Impulsive and instinctive behaviour certainly means that, if reactions that are true to life are to be ensured, man's aspirations will have to be limited. All the same, the vital development of his forces will be strong enough to bring about a change of direction in marginal situations, even if this change is only very slight. It is therefore not out of the question that instinct may have passed through so many changes of direction in man that it has at last reached a point where he has become seeing. It is even possible to say that man's instinct is becoming conscious of man himself and capable of reflecting about his movement forward and of setting goals towards which he should strive. There is nothing to prevent us from calling this sort of behaviour hope. To do this is not in conflict with Gehlen's view

[2] A. Gehlen, Der Mensch. Seine Natur und seine Stellung in der Welt (Frankfurt a.M., 1960), p. 14.

[3] It is, unfortunately, impossible for me to try here to define more precisely instinct as inherited or innate behaviour or as an inherited or innate behavioural disposition for the purpose of preserving the species or of self-preservation which can be modified by learning and experience. This question is discussed, for example, in J. Eibl-Eibesfeld's Grundriß der vergleichenden Verhaltensforschung (Munich, 1967), pp. 30, 168, 178.

3—C.

of man's special position, nor does it contradict the Thomistic demand that the sensitive forces in man should be ordered by human reason.

## 2. Evolutionary Expectations of the Future

Human hope is often tied to phylogenetical development. Man, it is said, is faced with mutation. "After 2,000 million years of organic evolution, man has emerged as the only product still capable of advance. Man is evolution made conscious of itself, and it is through this new psychosocial process that man has the capacity to create his own future and, in large part, control the future evolution of the planet."[4] Any "permanent revolution" has the task of ensuring that this development is continued and is not left to chance. It is therefore important to our belief in the future to recognize that the results of phylogenesis are sufficient to throw light on the present state of the world and its prehistory. They do not, however, entitle us to plan further mutations which we may expect to take place. Our concern for the present must above all not be clouded by an over-enthusiastic expectation of a better future.

Even Teilhard's attempt to achieve a reconciliation between Christian teaching and scientific thought was to some extent illusionary. His aim was to show, in the light of the incarnation, the dynamism which formed the beginning, the middle and the end of the process of evolution. In his view, man is at present in the course of becoming fully adult. He is conscious of his possibilities and therefore has to respond to the great responsibility and the splendid urge to create himself. Man and his world are, Teilhard believed, on the point of making a great leap forward, comparable to the leap made from primordial matter to life. The question arises, however, as to whether what we have here is an illusion which is leaving reality too quickly behind. Evolutionary thinking cannot therefore be placed on the same level as hope, because hope does not have to answer for the past or for the future, but for the present.

[4] R. J. Nogar, "Evolutionary Humanism and the Faith", in *Concilium*, 6, 2 (June 1966) (American edn., vol. 16).

## II. Passion and Understanding

### 1. Passion and Impulse

Evolutionary expectations of the future are often based on the results of such sciences as biology, psychology and sociology. Their illusionary and often passionate characteristics are therefore all the more surprising. This state of affairs can, at least partly, be explained by psychoanalysis.[5] Psychoanalysis is itself an anthropological discipline which has contributed to man's evolutionary expectations of the future, but which makes it possible for human hope to be distinguished from human passion.

The word "passion" is used to denote man's propensity towards strong reactions and increased desires. It is an acquired way of directing energy. The motive and aim of possible behaviour are not necessarily given—in itself, passionate behaviour is blind. Love and hatred, joy and sorrow, courage and fear, longing and aversion, hope and discouragement can all be sustained by passion. In modern anthropology, however, the word "passion" does not play a very large part. This may be because Sigmund Freud transferred his main interest from feelings and sensations to the motives for these feelings and sensations. His search for the reason for human behaviour led him to assume the existence of unconscious impulses and ultimately to discover the unconscious. For various human modes of behaviour, such as thumb-sucking, play, competition, dependence on other people, sexual relationships and so on, he discovered corresponding motives or needs. He therefore took as his point of departure a basic impulse which could be expressed in different ways. This impulse was a biological factor and its aim was satisfaction. "Impulses are directed towards something, a person, a thing or an activity which helps to reduce tension. The object which satisfies hunger is food; the object which satisfies sexual desire is usually a person of the opposite sex."[6] It is, of course, true that the individual's environment often prevents him from achieving satisfaction and relaxation, both of which are required by the impulse. In this

---

[5] S. Freud, "Psychoanalyse und Libidotheorie", in *Gesammelte Werke XIII*, pp. 209–33; "Das Ich und das Es", in *Gesammelte Werke XIII*, pp. 235–98.

[6] K. Menninger, *Das Leben als Balance* (Munich, 1967), p. 113.

case, the need may increase until it becomes desire. The impulse may eventually become so strong that it insists on being satisfied without regard to the existing reality. In that case, although the basic aim of the impulse is to preserve and to develop life, it becomes destructive in its effect.

In the case of animals, instinct sets protective limits to the insistent demands of impulse. In the case of man, on the other hand, the instincts are reduced and the goal towards which his impulse is moving is more ambiguous and less firmly fixed than in the case of animals. His impulse can be governed and directed. This gives rise to chance and even danger in man's life. Human passions are secondary structures, resulting from the effects of the outside world, social norms and, of course, the demands made by man's impulses. The outside world and social norms either inhibit the satisfaction of man's impulses or else direct them into definite channels. This does not, of course, take place without some conflicts, which contribute towards an increase in the strength of the impulses and bring about a change in its direction. Passions are therefore the result of unsatisfied impulses. The earlier and the more frequently conflicts occur, the more strongly are passions linked with the structures of human character.

The question inevitably arises here as to whether there is any authority which can have a corrective effect on already established structures of human character and can direct passionate impulses. The absence of any establishment of the impulses by the instincts means that there is a demand for an authority to set goals for the organization, direction and gathering together of man's impulses. Since this is only possible as a result of an understanding of a meaningful whole, there must also be an understanding of the movement of life forward into the future. Everything else would result in self-destruction. To define this understanding more precisely and to determine how much experience and presentiment it contains is less important than the fact that it forms part of the human attitude which assents fully to the future in present activity.

## 2. Expectation of the Future as a Substitute Satisfaction

Modern anthropologists must take very seriously the findings

of psychoanalysis concerning possible ways of satisfying by substitute the demands of impulse. Such unsatisfied impulsive desires
are not simply ultimately directed towards the future. Robes-
pierre's statement may be quoted as a typical example of misguided longing for the future. "O posterity, sweet, tender hope
of all mankind, you are no stranger to us. We defy all the blows
of tyranny for your sake. Your blessedness is the prize we seek
in all our painful battles. We are often in need of your consola-
tions when we are discouraged by the difficulties that surround
us. We entrust you with the task of accomplishing all our endeavours and we place the fate of all generations of men still un-
born under your protection. Make haste, O posterity, and let the
hour of equality, justice and happiness sound!"[7]

Psychoanalysis can certainly help us to see how illusions arise
from man's flight from reality. Man can, up to a certain point,
delay satisfying the demands made by his impulses, but they become more and more urgent and insistent. In the resulting
illusion, his psyche then makes use, as it were, of an artifice by
offering a substitute for unfulfilled satisfaction in the future. This
better future becomes a consolation for an unsatisfied present.
Man seeks flight from reality in a dream of a better future. This
results in his delaying the satisfaction of his impulses by making
use of his orientation towards the future. Since illusion—it
would be possible to speak here of "passionate hope"—presents
itself as optimistic and idealistic, it gives the impression of fully
consenting to and promoting life. Ernst Bloch has shown clearly
in his work on hope, *Das Prinzip Hoffnung*, how many different
aspects this "passionate hope" has always had and still has. Bloch
has called hope the human emotion of expectation directed
against fear and anxiety. Hope directs this emotion towards a
wider sphere and becomes a passion as soon as the whole man
throws himself into this emotion.[8]

Psychoanalysis enables us critically to assess the illusion of
pseudo-messianism in all its various forms. Wherever "passionate
hope" is active, man is orientated towards goals which do not
correspond to reality. Expectations which are not directed

[7] E. Fromm, *Jenseits der Illusion* (Zürich, 1967), p. 66.
[8] E. Bloch, *Das Prinzip Hoffnung*, Wissenschaftliche Sonderausgabe
(Frankfurt a.M., 1968), I, pp. 77–84.

towards reality must be regarded as the outcome of psychic processes in search of substitute satisfaction. The impulse urges man forward, but, since this impulse can be governed and directed, man can direct it away from satisfaction in the present and towards substitute satisfaction in the future. He lives in the present, but his thoughts are always in the future. The present is sacrificed to the future and a whole generation may be enslaved so that a future generation may live in freedom, equality and justice. In the religious illusion, heaven is often used as a substitute for the absence of real happiness here on earth and the compensation for a lack of interest in the present is a deep longing for future bliss. Our contemporary belief in the future and in human progress can, in many respects, be compared with the chiliastic movements of previous ages, the members of which have all had a fervent expectation of a "reign of a thousand years" in common. This belief in the future, as a psychic phenomenon, also resembles psychological depression, which is based on the same impulsive mechanisms. It is certainly true, of course, that the person suffering from depression does not dream of a future paradise, but of a past paradise. His depression can only be overcome when he is able to release himself from his longing for childlike security or, to express this in Freudian terms, when the unconscious demands made by his impulses have successfully been made conscious and have been subordinated to his reason. His actions will then no longer be governed by his impulses, but by the conditions of reality under which these actions take place. Man therefore has to use his reason to verify whether or not his activity is in accordance with reality. Although hope is firmly based on man's powerful movement forward into the future, it clearly cannot be passionate, but has above all to be understanding.

### III. The Primacy of Understanding

#### 1. *The Function of Hope*

It is not enough for man simply to keep alive—he has to know the meaning of his life. From what has been said so far, we could define hope as an attitude which directs man's striving or his impulses towards a rational future goal that is worth attaining.

This goal must therefore be conscious and rational. Since hope must be guided by an insight into the conditions which determine man's life, it is clearly the task of human understanding to exercise control over this hope. Man's vital forces are, of course, preserved together with all the structures of his character which gather his impulses together and direct them along definite paths.

Man's thinking keeps him open to the future and sets goals towards which he can strive. His character, on the other hand, may be regarded as a behavioural structure in which certain habits and attitudes have been stabilized. It represents the continuous and preserving element in man. Man's understanding, in other words, his capacity to make the impulse that is directed forward into the future, is the developing element in man. It is this understanding which constitutes the very essence of human hope.

Character and hope cannot be separated from each other. They represent the stabilizing and the dynamic elements of human life, which are mutually complementary in their polarity. The preservation of life is only possible when the future is guaranteed, in other words, when life is developing. Character comes from the experience that there is a meaningfully ordered life. Hope, on the other hand, presses forward from an understanding of the total reality to give meaningful form to life. It is not exactly the same as optimism, because optimism is not realistic and tends to make obstacles harmless. Hope, however, includes insight into the previously given reality and a powerful urge to make use of new possibilities and to avail itself of all the opportunities provided by the present to seize hold of the future.

The more complicated the world becomes, the more totally man must commit himself to the task of giving it meaning and form. One is bound to agree with Erich Fromm's statement that a future world will only be called into being when a new man comes into being—a man who regards himself as a citizen of the world and who, as such, directs his thinking towards life as a whole and towards mankind as a whole. If he is ever to live like this, however, man must learn to use his reason so that he will be able to recognize the illusory nature of most human ideas and press forward towards the reality.[9] In this sense, human reason is

[9] E. Fromm, *Jenseits der Illusion, op. cit.*, pp. 202–4.

not a collection of principles and truths, but a human force which is strong enough to embrace the future, a human attitude of hope. Man's chance of survival depends on his being able to control the forces of nature. One question, however, still remains — why is there life at all? What is the ultimate mystery of the force that preserves and sustains life and impels it forward?

## 2. Christian Hope

Hope is generally rooted in the power of the living being to develop. What, then, is the special characteristic of Christian hope? Whatever it is, Christian hope must have the same psychic structure as all human hope. It must be an understandable hope, that is, it must be possible to verify it against reality. It is therefore more of a task and a challenge than a gift.

Christian hope is tied to a particular goal and is determined by the history of God's activity with man acting together with him as his partner. This partnership in action was, of course, perfected in Christ. We speak of the activity of God and man together when man gives his assent to the creative basis of reality and acts in accordance with this. His relationship with the origin is less decisive here than his orientation towards the goal. The goal of Christian hope is the salvation of the world and more immediately the unity of mankind which can be achieved by man's unity with God. Christian hope is the attitude which directs man's forces and energies towards this goal. It is distinguished from an illusionary expectation of a better future by the fact that its strength is not derived from irrational demands made by human impulses. It is far more challenged by man's situation and, like any other service to mankind, confirmed by experience. Every service to mankind is, after all, not only experienced as meaningful — it can also be verified in one way or another.

Finally, the strength of Christian hope is derived from the experience that everyone who tries to live according to the spirit of Christ has. It is therefore not an inactive waiting for eternal happiness in the future, but action here and now in the present. It is based on the experience that love is an unconquerable force in the world. Man experiences love as something that creates unity and concludes from this experience that the goal towards which his hope is directed is attainable. In hope, man decides to make a modest contribution of his own to the work of perfecting and uniting mankind. What he achieves is enduring because he fashions his historical situation from the spirit of Christ. In the spirit of Christ, that is, in love, he gives his assent to the present in its significance for the future. Man's impulses and his passionate character lose nothing of their significance either in human hope or in Christian hope. In human hope, they are fulfilled by a philosophically founded understanding of a total reality, whereas, in Christian hope, they are fulfilled by the experience of effective love.

*Translated by David Smith*

Michel Demaison

# The Christian Utopia[1]

THE strength of a particular ethics is measured by its capacity to influence men, individually or in groups, to motivate their acts and to free them for what lies beyond those acts, namely joy. Now the ground seems to have gone from under the ethics officially put forward by the Church, which is quite a different matter from yielding ground. It no longer finds a place. This happens when an ethics is no longer able to take root in men's wills and unite them for a purpose which is both credible and practicable. It happens when an ethics eventually fails to instil a way of being and acting which can draw men's wills together for the advancement of human freedom and fulfilment. By that stage it has become an ethics directed at no one. Its topology is misguided, the force of its demands diminished, its criteria no longer reliable. It only subsists in the language of theory. That is why the treatises carry on long after the disappearance of the morals they are presumed to regulate. They do not die because there is no place for them; they flower in "the marvellous, smooth region of utopia".[2]

It is not therefore quite by chance, in my opinion, that theologians have readily begun to slip a new magic word into their discussions and publications: *utopia*. The fashion is no doubt dependent upon a number of factors. One, in particular, is difficult to elude: increasing conscious awareness of what was already a dim foreboding, namely that ethics no longer has a place, that

[1] This article is a slightly shortened version of one which appeared in *Lumière et Vie*, 95 (Nov.–Dec. 1969), pp. 87–110.
[2] An expression used by M. Foucault, *Les Mots et les Choses* (Paris, 1966), Preface, p. 9.

it is more and more difficult to fit it into the scheme of things. Once this impression is confirmed, it too is integrated into the rationalizations of learned discourse and thematized. Christian ethics is then presented as a utopia which both regulates and inspires acts, without it being seen that in this way it exposes its weakness.

If we are not to be deceived, we must throw light on what lies beneath the work (taking that word in its psychoanalytical sense) which theologians are doing in connection with the notion of utopia, and which some people, in another context, would call pottering about.[3] This article takes a preliminary look at the somewhat confusing notions of a Christian utopia.

## I. Traces of Utopian Language

Utopia is a complex entity. One can study it as a cultural phenomenon which is historically definable and documented in literary and artistic creations; as a method of research not unlike hypotheses in the experimental sciences; as a psychological reaction stemming from imaginary and rational sources; as an indispensable springboard for social progress. Each of these approaches involves ambiguity: according to one's presuppositions, utopia will either be the best or the worst of all possibilities.

It is thanks to Ernst Bloch that the word has been stripped of the pejorative connotations of futility and sterility which it has always had, even in its etymology. Bloch has made utopia into a major philosophical notion, defining its epistemological status and giving an ontological basis for its practical moral value: "to be a man means in effect: to have a utopia".[4] During the last twenty years or so, the word has gained more and more acceptance in philosophy, but has not yet acquired a set meaning.

Theology has been much less suspicious and seems to have

---

[3] Concerning the notion of pottering about (*bricolage*), cf. Claude Levi-Strauss, *La pensée sauvage* (Paris, 1962), pp. 29–33. It is dealt with by P. Ricoeur, "Structure et herméneutique", in *Esprit* (Nov. 1963), pp. 596–627, especially pp. 613–15. In relation to theology it is discussed by A. Casanova, *Vatican II et l'évolution de l'Eglise* (Paris, 1969), pp. 124 ff.

[4] Ernst Bloch, *Philosophische Grundfragen*, I (Frankfurt, 1961), p. 36. The title of this paper is "Zur Ontologie des Noch-Nicht-Seins" (For the Ontology of Not-Yet-Being).

endorsed it without too much quibbling. In what sense, exactly?
Is the word performing a new function or replacing another
notion which has fallen into disuse? Does its recent popularity
hide a sort of fear of emptiness? Up till now these points have
scarcely been examined, as if those who use the word were un-
afraid that they might be letting themselves be manipulated by
a terminology which they were using uncritically.

## Utopia as a Literary Genre

In the cultural heritage of the West, utopias appear relatively
recently as a literary genre. In general, they take the form of
treatises, narratives or dialogues; they are both literature and
philosophy combined, but fundamentally moral and political in
intent. The author's imagination constructs an ideal order of
nature and society, projects it on to another world and then often
describes it with a wealth of detail. Whether or not it is admitted,
the aim is thereby to exercise criticism of the existing order and
eventually to direct its transformation.

I am not here attempting a definition. There are a thousand
and one possible variations on the theme of the perfect organization of human happiness, many of which fall outside the scope
of literature: other arts and modern science, for example, further
extend the part played by the imagination in the dreams of
utopians, although the chimerical irrealism factor is tending to
disappear in the anticipations of science-fiction. Long before
Thomas More's *Utopia*, philosophers and poets had paid homage
to the myth of the just and happy city, beginning with Plato's
*The Republic* and *The Laws*.

A brief glance at the signs of a utopian current in history suffices
to highlight its absence from the biblical tradition: it has not
found expression as a cultural phenomenon recorded in either
documents or monuments.[5] It is useless to set off on a false trail
and hope to find books or passages in the Bible which come under
the heading of the utopian genre.

[5] The closest thing to it is the apocalyptic genre at the junction of the
sapiential and prophetic currents and turned towards the "revelation of
the divine mysteries" and "the time of the end". The sense of detail in
the descriptions and certain aspects of its social function remind one of
the utopian genre, but the differences are far more fundamental than these
similarities.

## Utopia and Eschatology as Literary Expressions of the Same Need?

We must begin from another angle. Utopian language gives an original shape to psychological and sociological constants relating to the human need to fashion an image for whatever is not known through the senses: man thus imagines the world outside his own as a town or an island, he abolishes duration in order to hold on to the definitive, he does away with obstacles and limitations so that he can touch on what is perfect, he lays the present moment open to the possible irruption of an ultimate which is always imminent. Only imagination gives these needs access to language. They then find a place in works where their different expressions combine to give universal human significance to the desire for happiness.

Our task is to examine whether, in Scripture, there are literary, cultural and juridical elements seeking to express these same needs, within a particular religious and social context, by promoting specific symbols and a specific rationality. In the exploitation of the themes of the Covenant and the Promise, in the activities of the prophets and the messianic movements, and in apocalyptical literature, is it not possible to see a parallel concern to that behind the utopias? The same question can be asked concerning the New Testament ideas of Kingdom, Church, Parousia, eternal life, the resurrection of the flesh, the last times, and concerning the whole of the book of the Apocalypse.

The answer necessarily requires a basic clarification from biblical experts. They will not fail to point out that these themes of the Old and the New Testaments are already endowed with and co-ordinated in an overall meaning: they come together to form what was later called eschatology. It is precisely from an eschatological angle that the Judeo-Christian revelation views the question of the perfect happiness of mankind. Grounded in exegetical analysis, the parts played by utopia and eschatology could then be assessed on the basis of scriptural texts and interpretation of them. The inquiry does not end with the Apocalypse. It must trace the manifestations of eschatology wherever the Gospel message has tried to find expression through the shifting layers of the imagination: in liturgies, monuments, the witness of mystics, images of the ideal City, the sporadic revivals of millenarianism, the messianic uprisings which are rooted sociologically in a situation of dereliction identical to that which accompanies numerous utopian inventions. Obviously these elements prove nothing in themselves. For each analogy and comparison, the differences and ambiguities must be explored in order that the respective meanings of eschatology and Christian utopia may be established. Before invoking documents or events of the past in support of his theses, the theologian must, therefore, ascertain the full significance attributed to them by the positive sciences.

Does Christian utopia, as an historical and cultural phenomenon, correspond to a reality which gives rise to a special mode of theological language? To settle this question here, one would have to assume that the tending towards the Kingdom was so univocal and specified that one could not fail to recognize the expression of it in any text or fact; one would have to assume that the utopian output which the human sciences are scarcely beginning to study was registered and immediately identifiable. Yet those are tasks still to be done and one must not prejudge the results.

At most one can point to the existence, in vestigial form, of utopian expressions in the literary, artistic and political history of the Bible and Christianity. Forms or fragments of forms testifying to a need which sought to be expressed and which is now called utopian, are like fossils which preserve the patterns of shells imprinted on stone of a completely different kind. If we are to discover whether utopia and eschatology are really two completely different things, we must continue our inquiry on another level.

## II. The Part played by Utopia

Utopia does not consist merely of projects for perpetual peace and futuristic plans for urban life. It is also a function of human behaviour, the processes and effects of which are observable in individual psychology but above all in collective situations and groups. We must, therefore, proceed to observe empirical patterns of behaviour which appear to be motivated by the utopian function.

## The Characteristics of this Function

A common factor is the ability to abstract from the world *as it is*, to break out of the apparently inescapable wall of things and causes, and to replace them with a plausible image of the world *as it ought to be*. Only the imagination is capable of taking this leap, whether one describes it as a tearing away from the sleep of conformism or as a jump into a fantasy world. But it does not do this just anyhow; the imagination also has its laws. I list them under three headings.

In the same way that a scientific hypothesis is the key element in experimental research, so the utopian imagination is the key element in the quest for happiness for all. It never ceases to find new combinations for re-linking old, but still live, images with man's latest idea of his own happiness; from there it goes on to build its ideal world. Because of its power to "make present" (*"présentifier"*) what is not really present, the imagination enriches consciousness with a way of approaching reality which is both stimulating and aggravating.[6] Like the hypothesis that supposes the problem is solved, it is in fact obliged to invent the means to solve it. Therein lies its *heuristic* aspect.

The utopian function does not exist in a vacuum. In general it is founded on an implicit or explicit criticism of a personal situation or of circumstances common to a number of men, and arises as a protest. This is the *critical* aspect of it: a sudden awareness of the intolerable, a dismantling of the excuses which preserve it, a refusal to let oneself be manipulated, this attempt to get away from what seemed inevitable and permanent takes very different forms according to the amount of freedom. But it is nevertheless a distinct stage in the psycho-sociological mechanism of utopia.

The third aspect takes into account both the rational and the

---

[6] The word *"présentifier"* is taken from Jean-Paul Sartre, *L'imaginaire* (Paris, 1940), p. 232. "There could be no realizing consciousness without an image-making consciousness and vice versa. Thus far from appearing a *de facto* characteristic of consciousness, the imagination emerges as an essential and transcendental condition for consciousness. It is as absurd to conceive of a consciousness which did not imagine as it is to conceive of a consciousness incapable of carrying out the *cogito*" (p. 239).

imaginary. Utopian language is neither poetry nor tragedy, nor is the utopian function pure fantasy released from all logic. It attempts to bring in the regulating role of reason in human action when it determines what should be done, and why and how it should be done, supposing that the perfect institutions of which it dreams did come about. This concern for orthopraxy, even though it betrays the dangerous freeing of the imaginary since it is wholly founded on an "as if", shows that man's practical and by implication ethical dimension can never be abolished. Itself necessarily dependent upon a prior practical situation, utopia tends to set up a new one: this is its *directive* role.

### The Utopian Function and the Leaven of the Gospel

Is this group of characteristics also to be found within the behaviour patterns and psychological reactions of believers?

From the "leave your country" addressed to Abraham to the "yes, my return is close at hand" of the Apocalypse, all the decisive initiatives inspired by faith appear as products of the desire to break out of the eternal circle of things "which are what they are" in order to pave the way for a new order obeying a new law. The imagination became vital and rarely has it functioned with such a wealth of inventiveness as when it had to map out the paths leading to the Kingdom of God, to prepare and hasten its arrival, to celebrate the glory which was to come. The irruption of the Christian imagination, acting as a stimulant, has influenced the course of history for entire societies.

So long as it does not become a collection of faded images, the imagination, borne aloft on biblical revelation, overturns readymade frameworks and gives back to the believer a glimpse of what is possible. He who understands how far one can be led by the "hypothesis" of love for one's enemies and sets out to verify it in practice is the most disturbing of men. He who applies the paradoxical logic of the beatitudes enters into the knowledge of the Kingdom in its essential mystery and in doing so reinvents life and rediscovers reality. Such people strip the good conscience of its last illusions, are not deceived by their own compromises and by the fraudulence hidden in every exercise of power, and can laugh at idols: in them the imagination of what ought to be is able to act on the present.

Just as utopia presupposes, for the sake of its own coherence, certain forms of behaviour among the members of the society it foresees, so too the gospel message only subsists by outlining a definite way in which the Christian is a man among men, acting with them. It even goes so far as to put this forward as an imperative, the new commandment. The new commandment regulates and gives direction to action: a role assigned to the utopian function. It seeks to promote within the contemporary contingent world a practical way of life which confirms the truth of the Good News: "You have died, you are risen, you are seated in heaven in Christ Jesus". Consequently, act according to what you are, that is, stripped of the old man, clothed in the new, and glorified. This, in a sense, is the ethical transcription of an anthropology which has been radically renewed. The law of charity is inferred from the characteristics of the transformed nature of the believer and then called upon to establish standards of behaviour in keeping with that nature. As a force for inventiveness, protest, and for indicating direction, the Gospel functions very like a utopia. Is it in fact precisely that, the Christian utopia?

If we mean that the idea of the end determines the act in its motives and its content, there is no need to invoke utopia: the classical theory of finality suffices. If we mean that the power of the image awakens the force of the desire, that the evocation of what is possible explodes dreary acceptance of what is ready-made and mobilizes dormant energy into revealing the riches to be found below the surface, then we are recalling an elementary constant in human life and especially in religious psychology and religious sociology. How else could we explain such phenomena as, for example, the behaviour of the early Christians awaiting an imminent Parousia, the attempts to create a Christian "social order", or certain current forms of revolt linking Gospel with revolution?

This much is already clear: the utopian function of Christianity rests upon the activity of the imagination which orders and stimulates a body of images to do with the coming of a Kingdom where the only law is love. This function acquires the role of revealing the unique end of human existence. It acts as a leaven which, by using the forces of desire, overturns the habits and

4—c.

values of the old world. It acts as the model for reformed customs and institutions.

## The Ethical Question

Here we are justified in taking a look at actual Christian practice. Does it, then, exhaust what the theologians claim as the meaning of the concept of utopia? For all the help it affords in revealing the part played by imagination and dreams at different levels of action, the utopian function never says whether a man *must* act in such a way or why he *must not* act in another. It remains just on the outer limits of the specifically ethical question. There is no point in holding this against it since it does not claim either to pose or resolve this question. But it is not pointless to ask why it cannot commit itself at the point at which morality is constituted. Its silence here is proof that utopia evolves outside the area in which the following question might arise: Why must what the Gospel commands the Christian be realized in practice? The other side of the question would be: Is the Kingdom of God the reproduction by the imagination of satisfactions projected on to the ideal, the whole of reality being nothing other than human needs struggling against their limitations, or not?

Theologians are forced to pose these questions by the use of the notion of utopia, even though they might wish to restrict it to its functional aspect. The *function* is inseparable from the *meaning* when it is a question of understanding the possibility and the specific nature of a life lived in accordance with the Gospel. Now, when we speak about Christian utopia, what are we doing if not seeking to give a particular interpretation of the Christian life?

### III. The Risks of a Utopian Interpretation

## Utopia as the Horizon of Human Activity?

It is not an arbitrary decision to interpret faith in terms of utopia. It is explained by the believer himself accepting the nature of the scheme of Christianity as conceived and justified. A way of life which freely sets its sights on the horizon of the Kingdom of God cannot adequately be measured and judged on the basis of the criteria of experimental knowledge which does not yield its full meaning. It demands another yardstick, incommensurable with that of science, but homogeneous with the faith dwelling in the active subject. This knowledge of faith is the only one capable of clarifying the ultimate meaning of the believer's actions.

But, as this knowledge bears only an analogous relation to experimental knowledge, it is understandable that, in today's cultural context, people prefer the word utopia. Is it not a question here of capturing the "surplus meaning" (*le surplus signifie*), to use P. Ricoeur's phrase, over and above the immediate sense, felt as a presentiment rather than imagined, anticipated symbolically because it cannot be incorporated in a system, wished for rather than possessed? In which case the utopia of faith would be the horizon of the promised Kingdom which, while remaining beyond practical, historical reality nevertheless casts over it the light of a definitive, perfect, ultimate meaning.

Can this point of view entirely avoid the criticism that it is ideology? It implies that one can define the essence of a way of life lived according to the Gospel by pointing to the relation to the utopia of the Kingdom as the characteristic which immediately impels recognition that this way of life is specifically Christian. The convenient term "horizon" severely risks covering a reality lived in such a differentiated fashion that it falsifies it by its generality; nothing is more easily falsified by univocal formulations than man's historical relation to the transcendent. The call to utopia is justified to the extent that "the horizon of the Kingdom" is determined not speculatively, but existentially, in relation to what man has been, is, and plans to be. Otherwise what significance could we attach to the claim to grasp the nature of a life lived according to the Gospel if this life has first been abstracted from the movement which makes faith incarnate in history? In my opinion, we will not find an interpretation of faith in this direction.

### Factors which make Room for a Christian Utopia

We must give up defining Christian life in terms of a utopia which ought to be put into effect. The only thing wrong is the fact that it never actually exists. The problem is to know subject to what conditions life lived according to the Gospel becomes meaningful. These conditions are realized when there is a dual tendency to accept history, humanly lived, as a manifestation of mystery, and mystery, which is believed in, as a force in the history which is lived. To bring out the unity in this dual tendency even more one could add that we must give historical reality to what we believe through faith *to be real* in such a way that the world can recognize it *as mystery*. Using the classical language of theology: the Incarnation is prolonged and Eschatology is proclaimed in one and the same process.

The indivisible binary rhythm of act and meaning, deed and purpose, which the believer also sees as the act of incarnation and eschatological meaning, defines the area within which something like the Christian utopia could emerge. This semantic area stretches between a fixed and a vanishing point; because of man's historicity, the fixed point, Jesus Christ, cannot now be restored as a simple fact attainable in the immobility of its past and the vanishing point, the eschatological Kingdom, is inevitably missed if it is not tied to the completion of the Incarnation event.

How can we see the utopian outlook in this tension, when utopia involves the construction in lengthy descriptions of the future of society, with past history sinking into silent oblivion? This dissimilarity is by no means superficial. If we examine it from three points of view, we shall be clearer as to the problems attached to a theological use of the idea of utopia.

(1) Utopia consists of an imagined ideal state of society as a whole and in detail, set in an undefined time and place. Even if it aims further, its essence lies in the art of constructing. Now, these constructions, however futuristic they may claim to be—or rather precisely to the extent that they aim at being pure products of the imagination—borrow their material from what is already to hand. They invent with the aid of what is old, nay, archaic. Basically, utopia conceals a secret fear of the future, the source of the unexpected, the unforeseeable, the completely new. Here it goes against eschatological meaning. For if Christians necessarily have made and continue to make themselves images of the Kingdom of heaven which they project into the future, they treat them merely as enigmatic, obscure, open images, such as the children of exiles might make of the country where they were not born. Having once said "all things will be new", they can

scarcely do more, except perhaps enumerate the relevant features of such a time and qualify each as new. This restraint is self-imposed because the not-yet of salvation is fundamentally different from everything imagined and wished for. Utopians can afford to be eloquent because they are engaged in reviving old need, archetype, symbol and dream potential. The believer is brief in order to remain free to create, to allow the new, which he awaits, to come to him through what he does.

(2) The critical function of utopia has been stressed. However, this criticism of the present is exercised from so far away that it is incapable of guiding the will to change what it evokes by stirring the waters of the imagination. Cut off from the constraints of knowledge and willing, the force of the imagination becomes powerlessness to act. It is inevitable that the moment of moral choice will be spirited away as soon as man's reconciliation with nature and with his fellow men is envisaged merely in terms of symbolical anticipation, as soon as every limitation is done away with without the force of its negativity being used.[7] It is the relation between utopia and time which is important. Imprisoned in and nostalgic for a mythical past, and safely caught up in a future outside time, utopia is never actually present when it comes to acting.

The Gospel, precisely because its final perspective is eschatological, refers us urgently back to the task at hand. It calls upon us to invent the actions which will give body to our willing of the Kingdom, taking into account the individual's objective circumstances and formation. The very acts of believing and hoping are conjugated in the present. Do away with the moment of moral decision and you will have destroyed the key to the Christian life; refuse to verify what is done in practice, and you will cause eschatology to become an illusion.

(3) For a few years now certain theological currents have been bandying the term "future" around. Not without reason. This emphasis is a product of the same change of mentality which explains the popularity of utopia: in the practical and intellectual

[7] There is a similarity here with the psychological attitude of "aestheticism". It has nothing in common, however, with artistic creation which only symbolically anticipates the reconciliation by playing with its essential limitation, matter and the laws governing it.

concerns of Christians, the centre of gravity is shifting from the past towards the future. But it is not clear that systematizations centred around the future and utopia satisfy the anxiety concealed in these concerns nor that they avoid the dangers of a new ideology. Is there not a tendency to relegate what has been accomplished in history to the rank of mere stammerings or abortive efforts? Like the ontology of "not-yet-being", the theology of the future could well end up by denying historical significance to the past and thereby rid itself at very little expense of responsibility for what has been determined by past actions. It would then be incapable of having a grasp of reality. And in fact the categories of future and utopia are not the only ones to possess the means of tackling events in themselves, analysing them theoretically and incorporating them in a way of life.

Through a *unique* event, and by weighing up the causes which occurred before it against subsequent events, we have the fixed and necessary point of any interpretation of the Christian life. Arising out of events and founded on them, faith is of its very nature equipped to grasp historical fact, to judge it and to be judged by it, to act in terms of it. Drawn out of history, faith becomes incomprehensible.

## Hope as the Object of Utopia

From all three angles examined above, utopia is seen to be blatantly guilty of "uchrony": as far as it is concerned, time and history do not exist, events serve to illustrate its theses and provide valuable points of reference for protest and extrapolation, but they have lost their substance and intelligibility. Consequently the believer is reduced to drifting aimlessly in a state of weightlessness. For history is the ground beneath him and the knowledge of Christ his force of gravity.

In fact, everything depends upon one's idea of faith. For the unbeliever, the word faith suffices to cast the whole affair into the realm of utopia, in the commonplace sense of fantasy and illusion. For the believer, the same word takes the whole affair out of the realm of utopia. The Christian believes that he cannot be in utopia because that would mean that he did not truly believe. Thomas More ended *Utopia* with the subtle and somewhat sad remark that he freely confessed there were many things which the Utopian people had which he would like to see established in the cities of his day, but that he wished it rather than hoped for it. The unbridgeable gap between wish and hope is that which separates utopia from faith.

The notion which, already in the Bible, sums up the authentic way in which the believer behaves in history has only one name, hope, because hoping is the act which links the present both to the fixed point of the historical Jesus and to the eschatological vanishing point. The Christian life cannot be reduced to an interpretation in terms of utopia inasmuch as it is *hope for what is believed* and not a wish for what is imaginable. In real life the line dividing the two is quite clear; it is not possible to confuse them. It remains true that both experiences, that of faith and hope and that of the imagination and wish, can coexist in the same individual.

Is it not precisely the reasons for this coexistence which theologians are seeking to understand when they talk of Christian utopia?

## IV. UTOPIA—A SOURCE OF STRENGTH

Once we are clear as to the inadequacies of certain uses of the term utopia, we can readily admit to its usefulness in other spheres: not as a hermeneutical focal point for a new interpretation of the Christian life but as a possible, and perhaps even indispensable, aid enabling faith and hope to be lived with true human meaningfulness and to be expressed intelligibly and in such a way that they can be communicated to others.

Traces of utopian structures can be located in the biblical writings and throughout the patristic and theological tradition. Certain initiatives on Christianity's part blend with the social repercussions of utopias. Some motives governing Christians' reactions bear some similarity with the roles of the utopian function. Is all this fortuitous or insignificant? Now that we have just reaffirmed the essential connection between faith and history, how could we, without contracting ourselves, reject this converging body of phenomena which have made up part of the history of faith? To break the ties between faith and its utopian halo would once again amount to a denial of its ability to find its own identity in anything other than a narcissistic stand-offishness. Fear of the new, irresponsibility towards the task at hand, inability to take on the responsibility of its past, to take only the negative aspects, surely make up part of its history and that of every believer. It is not as if Thamar, Ruth and Bath-sheba had no place in the genealogy of faith.

The presence of a utopian outlook surfaces with greater or lesser explicitness in the many ways in which the Gospel is lived and expressed according to the ways in which the believer's con-sciousness is structured; but it is always recognizable through revelatory facts and without it one could not explain all aspects of individual and collective forms of behaviour and the motives for them. This utopian outlook is a necessary part of the practical reality of faith inasmuch as a capacity for utopia is inherent in man's nature. I shall conclude by briefly pointing out how, on this level of practical reality, utopia acts as an aid or mediator for eschatological hope, and I shall do this by taking two poles of utopian activity: the liberation of the imagination and the will to rationalize political affairs in their entirety.

### Truth delivered up to the Imagination

Apart from the functions it performs, the imagination is valu-able and significant in itself. It is the vital medium in which symbolic activity flourishes: this is what makes the liberation of it in utopia a necessary mediating element in Christian life. Faith only becomes a humanizing commitment for he who symboli-cally fills the gap between his words and deeds and the hoped-for Kingdom. Now, this symbolical activity is at its highest point when it is rooted in the typically utopian need to evoke an ideal order of relations between men. And so, by exploiting indirect knowledge of myth, allegory and symbol, it tends to re-establish the psychical and ethical balance threatened by the totalitarian nature of other types of knowledge. Faith is not exempt from the need to "harvest" meaning wherever it can be found, includ-ing in utopian fields. What would have become of the Gospel if it had been transmitted solely through the documents of the magisterium and the treatises of theologians?

The liturgical celebration of the Christian mystery is without doubt the special area in which the part played by utopia is developed. In the first place, the indirect means of knowledge and communication abound: space, song, imagery, ritual, sacraments. But more than that, the process which gathers these various elements together realizes a sort of anticipation of eschatology, not now in the form of an illusory and demobilizing "as if", but by proclamation and attestation, in speech and in living gesture, of the symbolical presence of the not-yet of the Kingdom in the celebration being carried out.

However one chooses to express it, man's relation of dependence on the ultimate sets the imagination to work. When this ultimate presents itself in the shape of happiness to be distributed among many, dependence involves the construction of utopias.

### Political Utopias and the Kingdom of God

Imaginary representations of eschatology cannot eliminate political aims: the Kingdom of heaven, the City of God, the heavenly Jerusalem, the Body of Christ, all these are themes which envisage the elect in entirely new forms of relationship. Although it is useless to try to grasp the inner coherence of this order of things with our human concepts, nevertheless the coherence does exist with its own logic and rationality. This is doubtless what we call grace or charity.

The political dimension of the ultimate fulfilment of all things is witnessed by the absurdity of the notion of a single, individual salvation, by the permanent communion between members, the joy shared by all, reference to a principle of unity, the exaltation in each one of us of unexploited personalizing forces. The believer cannot want to encounter God without at the same time wanting all of that; that is why these requirements are preserved even in the most highly developed visions and images concerning eschatology. Politicians themselves cannot completely do without some concession to the imaginary in their ambitions to rationalize relations in a collective body. This is precisely the unique contribution which utopias make.

Utopia is thus vital in ensuring that hope of the Kingdom also influences those factors whose job it is to give imaginary expression to the political dimension of all human reality. This approach will always have a place within the eschatological perspective of the Gospel. This is possible because the ultimate impinges on reason via indirect forms of knowledge of which utopia is a classical example; it is necessary because eschatology severed from its political and social overtones is no longer Christian.

When they prevent eschatology and political affairs from setting themselves up in two self-sufficient camps and when they really uphold this severe tension between them, Christians are creating a situation in which the ethics of the Gospel can operate and theologians can then join them in the same struggle. The imaginary expression of the completion of this growth, the resolution of this tension, is the job of utopia. If you like, herein lies the inevitable Christian utopia.

But, to tell the truth, there is so much to be done to ensure that we do not flee the tension, to be open to its demands at every level, and it is so difficult to recognize the authentic advance of the Kingdom and to seek together for always provisional solutions, that I wonder whether the urgency of it all must not usually lead Christians away from the paths of utopia. As for theologians, when they have completed their work for the week, then let us grant them the right to turn into utopians on Sunday.

*Translated by Jonathan Cavanagh*

Juan Alfaro

# Christian Hope and the Hopes of Mankind

## I. Existence and Hope

MAN lives in so far as he has aspirations and plans, that is to say, in so far as he hopes. At his deepest level he is called upon to realize himself in the future.[1] Hope is present in all the fundamental dimensions of human existence, namely, in man's awareness of himself, in his freedom, his historicity, his temporality, his relationship to the world and to others. In hope the mystery of man as "finite spirit" ("incarnate spirit") is revealed.

The primary factor constituting the absolute originality of human existence is man's awareness of his own ego in its uniqueness; in this awareness each man grasps the immediate reality of his own being. But through this same self-awareness man is conscious of being only incompletely present to himself, of being not fully coincidental with himself; he can only be present to himself through contrast with what is not himself, that is to say in the encounter between his subjectivity and the objective. Self-awareness is immediate experience of man's spiritual being (his positive side) and of his non-being (finiteness, negativeness). From man's joint undivided awareness of his own being and his own finiteness springs his radical anxiety, *based* in his spirit (his presence to himself) and *conditioned* by his finiteness: man's essential tension towards his own fulfilment. Man carries within his awareness of himself an *a priori* aspiration to be his own individual and incommunicable self, to realize his own unlimited

[1] Cf. E. Bloch, *Das Prinzip Hoffnung* (Frankfurt, 1963), p. 2.

identity.  He feels the absolute imperative force of the call to realize himself in the successive and irreversible acts of his own freedom.  Awareness of how fragile this liberty is makes him uncertain of realizing himself and poses the inevitable risk that his existence will fail.  This is a call to hope, to a confident leap into the future.  Without this permanent call to hope human freedom would remain paralysed.  Hope is, thus, a transcendental dimension of human existence; it is inscribed in man's fundamental structure as "finite spirit" (*"transcendental hope"*).

Man can only exercise his will to be more truly himself through his activity in the world.  The world offers immense possibilities to match his unlimited aspiration.  By transforming the world man perfects himself, grows in freedom and self-awareness, and becomes more truly himself.  The task of transforming the world is inseparable from his absolute responsibility for perfecting himself; it is a mission entrusted to him, not just a result of the instinct for preservation or progress.  But man never fully realizes himself in any free decision; no achievement in his transformation of the world represents the final stage: he goes beyond the decision and the achievement in the very act of accomplishing them.  His capacity for hope always proves larger than his hopes in isolation; his future inevitably transcends all his concrete realizations of himself.  An insuperable disparity exists between his unlimited aspirations, which drive him to act, and the results of his activity in the world.  Human existence is a continual process of going beyond oneself; if this were not so, freedom would be condemned irremediably to the impossibility of making a decision.  Man's actions on the world contain within their own dialectic the impossibility of fulfilment in this world; his fundamental aspiration to be more truly himself transcends this world.  In his transcendental hope man catches sight of a future which he is incapable of creating with his own resources: a future which could only come to him as grace.

Human hope involves a community.  Each man, within his awareness of his own ego, is confronted with "other egos".  Man's existence is not solipsistic; his social dimension is as essential as his personal dimension.  "The other" is not something useful to me or an instrument for the advancement of the community.  His presence makes an absolute demand on me and on all men for respect and love. For this reason, as I must hope for myself, so must I for him and he for me: we must hope for all of us. This call to hope, which is both common to and yet higher than all of us because it transcends each and every one of us (each person representing an absolute value for all the others) reveals the basis which is common to and yet higher than all men: the call of a transcendent future.

"What must I do?", "What must I hope for?" are, according to Kant, the two questions basic to human action.[2] Would not simply "What must I hope for?" be even more concise? For hope emerges in man's consciousness as a call, a summons to take the radical and totalizing decision of existence. Whether he likes it or not, every man must opt either to open himself to the un-limited aspirations of his spirit for his own fulfilment (which he cannot achieve by what he does in the world) or to restrict himself to the inevitably limiting field of worldly expectations. This is man's fundamental option; in making this choice he decides to define the meaning of his existence: fulfilment as gift or autonomous self-realization without fulfilment. Every man lives either as one whose hopes are limited to this world or as one who hopes fully.

## II. Death as the Frontier for Hope in its Personal Dimension

Any interpretation of existence which leaves death out of ac-count is fatally non-existential, because death is the supreme possibility of existence: to exist is to go to meet one's death. Death gives human existence its decisive and irreversible character; for this reason death confronts man with the fundamental question about himself.

By madly burying himself in everyday hopes and concerns (i.e., by living as if he had not to die), modern man trivializes death; but he fails to realize that by the same token he makes life trivial too. Existence cut off from death is paradoxically existence cut off from oneself. Any attempt to bury death beneath the growing pile of worldly hopes is doomed to failure: it is useless to look for "life insurances" against the certainty of death. Every man is conscious of the certainty of his own death: he experiences the

[2] I. Kant, *Kritik der reinen Vernunf*, A 804–5.

radical insecurity of his existence, his creaturely finiteness, his own nullity. Death is present in us as our inevitable destiny and as a continual threat. By being present in anticipation it makes all our existence, decisions, acts in the world relative: whether we like it or not, it places an absolute final limit on our worldly hopes.

Death is as personal and untransferable as is man's awareness of his own ego: everyone lives his own life, everyone dies his own death. It reveals to each man the depth of non-being hidden within his own being. But it is precisely in this negative side of himself that each man discovers the deepest level of his existence. In death he experiences his total inability to save himself through his own resources, and the destruction of the fatal illusion of his own self-sufficiency. He cannot make the crossing to an ultra-mundane existence on his own, nor guarantee its existence with evidence supplied by his own reason. He has no option but to let himself be carried along by death to death, to let himself die (the experience of his supreme passivity). His intramundane existence crumbles totally. He has reached the frontier of the unverifiable, of absolute silence (stripped of all his images): where is he going? Man's anguish in the face of death arises from his spirit's awareness of itself, and its affirmation that he exists in the light of itself. He cannot stifle the desire to live, being unable to suppress his self-awareness; he cannot resign himself to sinking into nothingness, because he cannot resign himself to the loss of consciousness, which is his last refuge. If death were the absolute end, all human existence would tend towards absolute non-being, that is to say, it would be sustained by nothingness. But man's consciousness excludes negativeness as the ultimate level of its being; because it bears within itself the self-enlightening experience of its own being.

In its very proximity to nothingness death is, thus, a frontier of the transcendent, a radical call to take the decision of hope. Being totally unable to render his existence secure, man can only hope for the gift of a new existence. Death presents man with the option between an autonomous existence, limited to its possibilities in this world (a choice which is fundamental, whether it takes the form of heroic or fatalistic despair, of nausea at living, or an alienated existence ignoring death), and a brave open existence trusting in hope of a transcendent future. Death, then, is a frontier for man's freedom in the option it places before him between hoping and not hoping beyond the scope of this world. And because death is permanently present in human existence, the whole of life is a frontier of hope. In the response he makes to "transcendental hope" each individual interprets his own existence (every interpretation of one's own existence involves a choice) and decides its definitive meaning.

III. HISTORY AS THE FRONTIER OF HOPE IN ITS SOCIAL DIMENSION

Human existence is more than just personal. As a member of the human community, each man is called to take part in the transformation of the world and in the creation of history. His existence is bound up with mankind's advance towards its future; thus the question of mankind's future affects the meaning of each individual's existence: humanity's future is mine as well. Modern man is increasingly more aware of his social projection into the future.

Through its achievements over the centuries, mankind has grown in socialization and domination of nature. But it would be utopian to think that this process will one day rid us of human antagonisms and achieve a perfect harmony between individual freedoms in an ordered community (the tension between man's relation to himself and his relation to others [*autocentrismo y heterocentrismo*] appears insuperable) or that it will achieve a balance between mankind's aspirations and the world man transforms. What man does with the world is inevitably objectifying, that is, it creates new possibilities for transforming the world. In the very moment of action, the result slips from man's subjective grasp and becomes an object, "thingified" before him. The "subject-object" ("man-world") dichotomy is automatically reestablished in the process of man's acts in dealing with the world; it cannot be eliminated within the reciprocal relationship of "mankind–world transformed by it". Moreover, the permanence of this dichotomy is a prerequisite for human activity in any sense. The moment the world becomes completely under man's control it would be merely his plaything, lacking in any value to him. He will have nothing to seek or create in the world;

he will have built himself a perfect prison for his freedom. From being the manipulator of the world he will, paradoxically, have become the victim of his own manipulation; mankind, wholly adapted to the possibilities of the world it has transformed, will have reduced itself to the level of the perfect "robot".[3]

It is consequently vital to accept that human activity contains the implication that it is impossible for mankind to find its definitive fulfilment in its work of transforming the world. Mankind could carry on creating new provisional futures indefinitely, only to see each one replaced by the very fact of being attained. Mankind's future, if there is one, cannot be his doing. History's future must of necessity be, not an historical future, but a future transcending history, something "totally other" foreseen in the historical process itself. Within its own sphere the history of mankind never arrives at its fulfilment.

It is useless for mankind to rely on an unlimited survival in the world. Not only because it amounts to a gratuitous hypothesis (which is unverifiable, undemonstrable, and, what is more, seriously undermined nowadays by the possibility that mankind will destroy itself), nor principally because it fails to solve the grave question of each individual's disappearance in death and the successive disappearance of every generation of men (neither is a human person an anonymous moment in his generation, nor is this generation purely a preparatory phase for the following one). But above all because a hypothesis of this kind leaves unanswered the basic question of the meaning of the historical process itself. Why cannot mankind act in this world without for ever transcending everything it accomplished by its actions? Why are creating history and transcending it one and the same thing? What mysterious force impels mankind for ever "further forward", or rather, endlessly attracts and yet escapes him? If one looks for the answer to this radical question solely within the closed circuit of the reciprocal immanent relationship "mankind-

---

[3] Cf. K. Rahner, "Marxistische Utopie und christliche Zukunft des Menschen", in *Schriften zur Theologie*, VI (Einsiedeln, 1965), pp. 77–88; J. B. Metz, "Gott vor uns. Statt eines theologischen Arguments", in *Ernst Bloch zu ehren* (S. Unseld, Frankfurt, 1965), pp. 227–42; M. Moltmann, "Il futuro come nuovo paradigma di trascendenza. Un tentativo", in *Riv. Internz. de Dialogo*, 2 (1969), pp. 6–25; "Zukunft und Transendenz", in *Intern. Dialog. Zeitschr.*, 2, 1 (Jan. 1969), pp. 2–13.

world", one will be forced to admit that mankind is utimately ruled by the impersonal, iron law of the evolution of the world; man is reduced to a mere product of nature's immanent dynamism and his only *raison d'être* is to contribute to the working out of this dynamic force. But can man understand his awareness of his creative liberty simply as a privileged instant in the fatal deterministic evolution of the world? Mankind has only one alternative: that of understanding itself as called to hope in a transcendent future which it cannot itself create but which it can receive as a gift. History is then revealed as a new frontier with transcendence, that is, as a frontier for the option to hope. In the acts whereby it creates history mankind must opt between a becoming with no future (a purely immanent, intramundane becoming) and a becoming open to the gift of a transcendent future.

## IV. Christian Hope in its Personal Dimension

Christian existence is characterized by the social and personal qualities of faith, hope and charity, closely linked together and centred on God's revelation-gift of himself in Christ. Faith looks first to what God has already done in Christ for the salvation of mankind and the world; only within faith is it possible to understand hope and charity, because only in faith is it possible to know the mystery of Christ and man's sharing in him. Hope, which looks above all towards the future fullness of God's revelation in Christ, gives to faith and charity their eschatological dimension. As communion between God's life and man's and between men in Christ (that is, as the love of God fulfilled in love and disinterested service of men), charity constitutes the unifying bond between faith and hope, and the element which perfects them; from charity Christian existence receives its unity and its ultimate meaning.

The essence of Christianity (its "question of being and non-being") lies in God's personal presence in history, namely in the personal, divine character of the man Jesus. In Christ's incarnation, death and resurrection (three immanent stages of one and the same mystery) God has accomplished and revealed his definitive act of salvation; the destiny of mankind and of the world to

5—c.

share with him in God's eternal life has been irrevocably established in Christ.[4]

Christ is the "eschaton" before all things in himself and for himself. His existence in history was directed in itself to transcending history (the identity between the crucified and the risen Christ: Acts 2. 36; 3. 13; 4. 10). The fact that he was genuinely "a man like ourselves" implies that he was destined to die; his personal, divine being ensured that he would triumph over death: as Son of God made man Christ was destined to pass through death to life with God beyond history (Heb. 2. 10–18; 7. 24, 28; 9. 14; Acts 2. 24; Jn. 1. 14; 10. 15–18). The mystery of Christ contains the quality of being "once and for all" (Heb. 7. 27; 9. 12, 28; 10. 10, 12), that is to say, of being irrevocable and unrepeatable, of being definitively triumphant over sin and death.

As a member and as leader of mankind (the solidarity of the Son of God made man with all men), Christ is also our "eschaton" and the world's. His presence in history represents the beginning of the end of history; in him and through him all mankind (together with the world created by it) is destined to share in his glorious life beyond time (Rom. 8. 19–23, 28–30; 1 Cor. 15. 20–23; Eph. 1. 10; 2. 6; Col. 1. 15–18; Phil. 3. 21). This destiny is interiorized in man during his earthly existence by the gift of the Holy Spirit, who calls him to share in God's life; the presence within man of the glorified Christ through his Spirit is his guarantee and foretaste of the resurrection to come (Rom. 5. 5; 8. 11, 14–17; 2 Cor. 1. 22; 5. 5): already man receives "eternal life" from Christ (Jn. 3. 36; 6. 40; 10. 10, 28; 1 Jn. 3. 15).

As supreme fulfilment and revelation of God's saving love of all men, Christ's death and resurrection invite a boundless hope; the Cross is immensely significant for our hope (Rom. 5. 8; 8. 31–39; Eph. 1. 7; 2. 4; 1 Tim. 2. 3–6; 4. 10; Jn. 3. 6; 1 Jn. 4. 9–16). The presence of the Holy Spirit in the believer enables him to understand the mystery of Christ as a call to trust completely in this God who has manifested himself in Christ as the God-Love (Rom. 5. 1–5; 8. 14–17; 15. 13; 1 Jn. 4. 8–16). Man's response to this call of God's love in Christ is Christian hope: a radical decision to take one's existence into one's own hands

---

[4] Second Vatican Council, Dogmatic Constitution on the Church, n. 48.

boldly in order to abandon oneself unconditionally to God's promise. The believer is conscious that he is a sinner and that he is destined to die; he knows that his fragile freedom represents an unavoidable risk to his salvation and that faith itself will not allow him to make human calculations as to his personal fate after death; he knows and lives the drama of his existence. But he conquers this uncertainty (which is always a temptation for him) in the boldness of his total surrender of himself to God's saving word in Christ. Christian hope is "existence in exodus", that is, a going out of oneself, renouncing any guarantee of salvation provided by human reckoning, in order to trust solely in the divine promise: a breaking of the moorings of all assurance in oneself and in the world, and a tossing of the anchor into the bottomless depths of the mystery of God in Christ. In this radical surrender of himself to the grace of God in Christ (which constitutes the very nucleus of Christian hope), the believer carries out his gift to God in reply to God's love for him; he accepts and appropriates to himself the grace of God in Christ. In the act of hoping he lives the experience of being loved by God; he is conscious (with an a-thematic knowledge) of God's love for him. This is the certainty of Christian hope: certainty that God is for me the God of grace, a certainty lived (not reflected) in the very decision to hope; a certainty which grasps the promise and thus tends towards the salvation to come. "Justification by faith" means "salvation in hope" (Rom. 5. 1–5; 8. 24–25).

## V. CHRISTIAN HOPE IN ITS SOCIAL DIMENSION AND IN RELATION TO HISTORY

The Christian hopes for salvation, not only for himself but also for the human community and for what man accomplishes in the world, history. The basis of his hope (the death and resurrection of Christ) has universal meaning. Christ glorified is Saviour and Lord of all men (Acts 4. 12; 10. 36; Jn. 4. 42; 12. 32); in him the whole of creation finds its central support and final purpose (1 Cor. 8. 6; Eph. 1. 11; Col. 1. 16–18; Heb. 1. 3; Jn. 1. 3). Christian hope is not authentic if it lacks a universal dimension; in its deepest reality it includes man's gift of himself to the God-Love, and the love of God is inseparable from the love of men

(1 Jn. 4. 7–12, 20–22). Charity, the fullness of hope, requires the Christian to hope for others as for himself, that is, to love his neighbour as himself.

For the Christian, the fact that mankind and its history are going towards a transcendent future is a mystery of faith, not a human conclusion or foresight. It is not man who with his own resources will carry history on to its definitive fullness. In so far as it is the work of man, history unravels itself in an indefinite succession of stages superseding one another. The Absolute Future is an unforeseeable gift which can only come about as Freedom and Grace: it is the mystery of God's self-communication in Christ; the believer looks towards him in hope. Christian eschatology is an eschatology of hope.

Because he believes in the death and resurrection of Christ (namely, in God's personal presence in history, in a Christ who is at once historical and metahistorical), the Christian believes that the man who is guided by the Spirit of Christ already experiences God's self-communication.[5] Every individual is called to share in God's life ("Christic existential"). The present reality of man's transformation through the Holy Spirit (the "already" of justification by faith) is a foretaste of the "not yet" of the hoped-for salvation. The presence of the grace of Christ in man directs his existence and his activity in the world towards the definitive fulfilment of mankind and of history. Man's transformation of the world is thus given an entirely new meaning by Christ's grace: in his response to God (faith, hope and charity) fulfilled in his relations with others and with the world (man's action in the world is not merely an expression of his being, but his authentic fulfilment), humanity "formed by Christ" (*cristiforme*), together with the world and the history inseparable from it, tends towards the Absolute Future, God. But Christ's grace is not something at man's disposal like an object or a force of this world, nor is it a means for his salvation; as God's self-communication in himself to man, it always transcends man, whose free acceptance is always a receiving of God's gift in hope. Thus it is God himself (Absolute Future, Future as Absolute Grace) who in giving himself to man brings mankind and its history towards

---

[5] Cf. E. Schillebeeckx, "Some Thoughts on the Interpretation of Eschatology", in *Concilium*, 1, 5 (Jan. 1969), pp. 22–9 (American edn., vol. 41).

their fulfilment. The history of mankind and the history of salvation are not identical; but the history of salvation takes place in man within his existence in the world.[6] It is man himself, together with his world transformed by him and his history, that is "now already" being saved by Christ. "He who is to come" is already coming: the Kingdom of God is arriving (Mk. 1. 15; Lk. 11. 20). The Christian awaits its definitive coming as the revelation of God in himself (the totally-Other) beyond all human foresight and imagery.

Far from alienating man from his mission of transforming the world, Christian hope stimulates him to carry out his intramundane task and integrates his commitment to the world in his responsibility before God and before men, who are his brothers in the firstborn among men, Christ. The Christian lives according to the hope (founded in faith) that man's action in the world will neither end in failure nor lose itself in an endless search for a fulfilment which will never come; his hope in a definitive fulfilment sustains him in his worldly activity. Moreover, the grace of the Absolute Future does not remove but on the contrary radicalizes his responsibility as an actor with a part in history (just as the gift of justification does not suppress but is on the contrary fulfilled in the free response of faith); the salvation of man and of the world come about in the dialogue between the Absolute Freedom of God in his self-communication to man and man's responsible freedom before the call of the God-Love. Charity, the fullness of hope, demands from the Christian a radical involvement in the tasks of the world for the good of mankind. Precisely in the fulfilment of his responsibility to mankind, the world and history, Christian hope anticipates the coming of the Kingdom of God in Christ.

[6] J. Alfaro, *Hacia una teología del progreso humano* (Barcelona, 1969), pp. 93–104.

*Translated by Jonathan Cavanagh*

Josef Goldbrunner

# What is Despair?

ONE CAN represent despair as a spider that has settled itself in the web of man's life where it kills everything with its poison. Both the spider and the web, however, are me. I turned turned against myself. I am in despair.

The web of human relationships has to be re-woven with threads strong enough to bear the tension, biological, psychological, personal and theological. We have to examine the conditions that bring about this despair. And finally, we must trace possible ways of mending the situation.

Today extreme despair does not infrequently occur in the sphere of religious experience. This seems to indicate that the industrial and technological culture is only now beginning to have its full effect on the human condition. From the point of view of salvation history this change might be described as a new phase in the way human nature (*sarx*) reacts to the Christian message (pneuma).

## I

One of the main lines on which human life develops is the relation between *"without and within"*. All kinds of events, both positive and negative, press themselves upon man from without, and we should understand how the intensification of the negative events leads to despair. Failures, disappointments, illness, loss of property, loss of relatives knock, one after the other, on the door of the "within" which cowers and shrinks before fate until it surrenders.

The end of such a chain of fatal events may well be despair.

With every misfortune man has to surrender a part of his life. Every time something has come to an end, and every time a relationship with the "outside" is cut off.

This creates isolation, loneliness, hopelessness within; there is no way out and there is no meaning in existence: "In so far as I am concerned, there is no more sense in life." Nothing is any longer wished for, nothing expected, nothing hoped for.

An enemy within has reared his head against the self, and here we have the situation of despair. In this inner world resistance, resiliency and the very ability to experience anything have petered out—everything "has already died", is dead. At the bottom of despair lies a death experience, or, rather, the experience of dying.

As we know from experience, the biological life-force can react to this situation in three ways. The reaction can be sheer resignation. All strength is gone, and whatever is still alive within lets anything happen to itself with a total lack of interest till everything comes to an end. The basic life-force is broken, and despair spreads like a frost which freezes the life out of everything. Resignation lets life vegetate till the last flicker of it has faded out.

It is, however, also possible for the basic urge-to-live to reassert itself, to turn its last strength against the self and to put an end to despair by suicide.[1] According to E. Ringel, however, 85% of these people are grateful if somebody saves them, which means that when the urge-to-live tries to short-circuit the process by suicide (although it can go through a long process of preparation), it changes into a pathological condition.[2]

There is, however, a third way that must be mentioned, even

---

[1] The suicide rate in the world today is about 1 in 10,000. The German Democratic Republic has the highest rate in the world: 2.9 in 10,000. See Klaus Thomas, *Handbuch der Selbstmordverhütung* (Stuttgart, 1964), pp. 9 and 32. In his *Neue Untersuchungen zum Selbstmordproblem* (Vienna, 1961) E. Ringel describes this last self-destructive impulse as an illness. Fifty per cent of those who commit suicide suffer from depression. K. Thomas (*ibid.*, p. 47) maintains that, subjectively, the man that commits suicide is practically never responsible, and that, objectively, "suicide is the last despairing cry of a lonely man", a cry left without the saving response from someone else. James Hillman, in his *Selbstmord und seelische Wandlung* (Zürich, 1966), wonders what the psychological meaning is of suicide (p. 50). I shall come back to this point.

[2] I have not gone into the factor of inheritance and its consequences. For the psychiatric aspects of suicide, see the relevant chapters in K. Thomas and E. Ringel.

if it occurs rarely at the biological level (and our argument is restricted here to this biological level), and this is a sudden regeneration. This would mean in the first instance that the experience of dying (i.e., the surrender of all that went before) has touched and transformed the urge-to-live. It is possible for man to change overnight in some unexplainable peace, to accept all that has happened and to turn to other things.

Should we say that, in such a case, there were biological reserves that had not been tapped in a man's relation to life up till then? Is it possible for the urge-to-live (and we mean the basic biological urge-to-live) to pull out of the kind of life led so far and to turn to a new way of life through some instinctive compulsion? But this would only be possible if the biological urge were not destroyed but re-vitalized.

In a man's consciousness such a regeneration would be experienced as unforeseen, wholly unexpected, as a gratuitous occurrence, a gift, or grace, something like a reversal or a leap. It must be frankly admitted that the sole biological aspect is no longer enough to explain such a happening, because regeneration through contact with the experience of death seems to imply a definite psychological aspect. In other words, man's biological aspect is constantly intertwined with the other aspects of human existence, and first of all with the psychological aspect of man.

## II

The interplay of the psychological forces in man can be presented in terms of "above and below". No doubt, the dimensions of above and below have been demythologized, that is, they are no longer cosmological dimensions. They retain, nevertheless, their anthropological validity, symbolized in man's stature, his feet standing on an earth that reaches out towards heaven.[3]

Man's biological urge-to-live has not only a physiological aspect but also a psychological one. This means that it has its roots in the vegetative sphere, that dormant primitive ground of the psyche, and is dependent on what happens in the conscious mind.

[3] For anthropological purposes one can use the image of the seed which pushes its shoot into the light and drives its root into the soil. See August Vetter, *Personale Anthropologie* (Freiburg, 1966), pp. 18 and 55 f.

Height and depth condition each other, and when the transcendent capacity of man loses its locus "above", there will be a corresponding loss of firmness at the roots.

The anthropological consequence is the collapse of the necessary tension between "above" and "below", so typical of contemporary man. These two poles are no longer related to each other. Man's mental life has degenerated into mere intellectualism and thrives on interminable arguments.

This can be seen in theology[4] as well as in sociology, where man seems to work in a kind of "germ-free thought-laboratory". Man has severed himself from his roots in the vegetative sphere. He can no longer steep himself in the rhythm of life in the soil from which he has sprung. He suffers from insomnia and many disturbances at the vegetative level.

This breaking away from the vegetative sphere may also explode in such phenomena as the hippies and their search for ecstasy, even with the help of drugs and psychedelic colours, so significantly linked with plants or flowers, i.e., vegetative things. To the "thought-laboratory" above corresponds the jazz-cellar or the crypt in a "vigil house" below.

With the loss of the cosmological dimension of above and below man has lost the original assurance of his ability to transcend as well as the ability to immerse himself in the unconscious rhythm of life at the vegetative roots of his existence. All this leads to a situation where life has become meaningless[5] and produces nausea.

And so we have again a collapse of a personal world, another experience of dying, and the spider of despair crawls out of its corner. Once again we have three possible reactions: resignation, suicide or sudden change, the last of which is of particular interest here.

[4] C. Münster, "Bericht von Drauszen", in *Existenzprobleme des Priesterbildes heute* (Munich, 1969): "The thought models of theology, which had their meaning and function in an earlier Christianity, are as alien to the faith as the atom models of classical physics are to the modern situation of this science" (p. 189).

[5] J. Herzog-Dürck, *Probleme menschlicher Reifung* (Stuttgart, 1959): "Meaninglessness is one of the most frequent symptoms of neurosis today, in contrast to repression, as was held formerly" (p. 13). E. Ringel holds that the meaninglessness of life is the main motive for suicide (*op. cit., passim*).

Let us take it that "above" and "below", "heaven" and "earth", find each other again. Would it not be possible that some third element emerged in the process, something that would act as a binding force?[6] In that case the job one has in life might become bearable again, the spontaneous desire for depth would not have to be driven into the cellar, intellectual life and the vegetative forces at the roots could again live together "within". If this happened in the psychological sphere, the "forecourt of the religious sphere", it might well lead to a "religious orientation".

## III

Some help for this sudden change, this jump away from despair through meaninglessness and nausea, can be found in a third guide-line that runs through man's life, namely the relationship between the impersonal and the personal. This transition from the impersonal world of intellectualism and logical argument to a world of persons, from "it" to "you", is like the breakdown of a defence mechanism, the surrender of one's self-protection, the acceptance of being defenceless. This breaking open of the bud to let the flower come out comes almost instinctively to the young person when he or she falls genuinely and personally in love; it works like a charm. But when the truly personal element is never called upon—and this seems to happen more and more—the actuation of the personal element becomes difficult.

The withdrawal into the impersonal, the sheltering behind "society", behind impersonal logic and rationalization turns everybody into an "it". There is then no personal contact between people apart from the "businesslike" contact between business partners. One might almost call the personal element the "lost dimension" of today. Everyone is locked up in his own prison, a prison which he is aware of but cannot put a name to.

This breaking apart of the "it" from the "you", the impersonal from the personal, again implies an experience of dying. The law of "dying in order to grow" seems to be written into the whole cosmos, the human cosmos included.

To surrender myself, to put myself defenceless into someone

---

[6] A. Vetter, *op. cit.*, pp. 93 f.

else's hands in total trust, to do this at the risk of being exploited and misused, all this grows into a true experience of dying as we grow older. The sudden change-over to a life with a new quality, the personal quality, is only possible by dying to the protective armour-plated world we have built around ourselves. A person who does not give his self away cannot break through his isolation, nor escape from the prison of meaninglessness, cannot open up, trust, ask, forgive, love.

Change, metamorphosis, renewal, resurrection—all these words picture what happens when an event bursts upon us and calls us forth, and the answer is not given by reason or some emotion, but by the personal self. This centre of my self is called upon, and then actuated and shaped by the response to this call. "Above" and "below" find themselves united again in me in a new way.

When such a man communicates he finds rationalization boring, and when he speaks he suddenly finds himself speaking in concrete images, and no longer in abstract terms. Imagination has been stirred into life, "above" and "below" have found each other in the centre, and the mental sphere is again in touch with the vegetative sphere at the roots. The possibility of a new life has been discovered, and despair fades away. Would it not be possible that this step from being the plaything of psychological mechanisms to the level of a personal existence could lead us into the "forecourt" where the conditions are created for overcoming religious despair?

Assistance, however, is essential to enable someone to leap on to the level of the personal, and this aid is a fellow man.[7] How far he can help can be seen in the therapeutic relationship between a psychiatrist and a patient as in a magnifying glass. The psychiatrist is not there so much to point out and to explain as to *enable*. Something goes out from the manner of his presence—and here lies the real secret of the efficient psychiatrist—something that works like osmosis or the reverberation of sound from a soundboard.

Without imagery, this means that his personally actuated existence, the quality of his being a "you", has the power to evoke

[7] For education to the personal life, see J. Goldbrunner, *Realization* (University of Notre Dame Press, 1966).

the personal element in the other. Minds can clash and stir each other up to argue things out, one will-power can try the strength of another, and emotions can become intense through mutual excitement. But the personal element, too, can influence the dormant, confused, immature or fear-ridden personality of another; it can call forth, invite, court.[8]

That such a personal call no longer touches everybody today (at least once in their lifetime), that man's personality is barely actuated today, and that he is not even capable of this actuation—all this explains why so often man remains desperately stuck in the workings of the psychological mechanisms.[9] That the personal sphere has become a "lost dimension" is one of the main reasons why so many can no longer cope with life and fall into despair.

From the point of view of salvation history one can see that it is part of the strategy of the powers of Antichrist to prevent the awakening of the personality of man by reducing people to a mere mass. The levelling down of people in the mass confuses the personality, crushes it[10] and so makes it unable to accept the Christian message from a personal God, and this is the next point.

## IV

Straight religious despair seems again to be linked with another guide-line in the web of human life, the line that leads from *presence* to *absence*.

God is no longer present. In some strange way one can still believe in him, but he does no longer exist, he is no longer real, has become a mere flimsy theory instead, without any power. He is even less than merely passive, he simply is not there.

[8] Cf. J. Hillman, *op. cit.*, p. 148: "The only instrument of the analyst at the time of analysing is his own person."

[9] In so far as psychotherapy does not integrate the personal quality in its image of man, unfortunately only pothers about in the psychological mechanisms, like a mechanic who tries to get the motor going again. He does not ask about the whither of the journey. This inability to see the "meaning" is the cause of many psychological disturbances. Cf. J. Goldbrunner, *Personale Seelsorge* (2nd edn., Freiburg i. Br., 1955), p. 88.

[10] The most frightening picture of this world has been given by George Orwell in his novel, *1984*.

And yet, the soul bleeds as through an additional wound in its wish to pluck somehow some certainty about him from somewhere. His absence causes pain and suffering. And one is afraid that this suffering will spread like a running sore and will attack the faith one still may possess. And slowly the spider injects its poison into man's consciousness.

In this situation of religious despair all that has been said so far comes into play, only more intensely: the three possible reactions (resignation, suicide, sudden change), the experience of dying, aid from outside. The various impulses are not only driven to the limit, but all the levels mentioned before—the biological, the psychological and the personal—flow together and reinforce all that lies behind this religious despair.

In this religious sphere resignation is so widespread that one can almost speak of a "general religious strike". These people could only be moved religiously if some terrible fate ploughed right through their accepted reality. Nevertheless, they, too, are still subject to the workings of the Spirit, are still covered by the praying community, and therefore are not abandoned, at least from this point of view. They exist on the fringe of the community, on one of the outer concentric circles (if one can apply this pattern to the Church); they belong to Christianity as the fringe belongs to a society or the polar sea to the globe.

Suicide out of religious despair would mean that the meaninglessness of existence has become total and every impulse to live is gone. "I have no desire left," says the tyrant in Bergengruen's novel of that title. There is nothing any more in the background of existence, and this nothing has its own peculiar lure for what still remains of the urge-to-live, just as the abyss draws those that cross the bridge over the abyss.

One certainly does not help these people by by-passing this particular form of despair. On the contrary, one should talk to them about the "meaning" of it, so that they become articulate about it.[11] In this "dangerous game", where the counsellor tries

[11] Cf. J. Hillman: "The analyst is less concerned with suicide as such than with helping the other to understand the meaning of such an option, the only option that demands the concrete experience of death" (*op. cit.*, p. 50).

to penetrate into this urge towards self-destruction, the only possible way out is that of the sudden change.

This sudden change to life with a new quality in the sphere of religion is called conversion, a turning back towards God. The pivotal point in the conversation (not necessarily the most effective, but more about that later) will be the absence of God.

"Absent" here does not mean the mere fact that God is not seen, but rather that he *cannot* be seen because the traditional religious images and ideas of God are not only useless but actually block the way to God.

Just as one cannot see the naked wall of a room unless one takes down the pictures, so the absence of God allows us to see the "naked Godhead" (Mechtilde of Magdeburg).[12] This is again a kind of experience of dying. Mechtilde, who was a mystic, used expressions like: "Lady Soul, you should be outside" and "In love, life and death are the same".[13]

This is the language of mysticism. In modern language one might say that we think and ponder right through the barriers of time and space (our modern space!), as if we were thinking right through the sound-barrier, and so through the zone of death, too. And this is a real kind of dying, not only for the intellect, but also for the imagination and in one's deepest feelings. This is a mysticism at the contemporary, natural level.

Such an experience may be compared to that of some Eastern monks who do their meditating among the rocks. Man sits in front of a wall of rock. There is no way out, neither to the right nor to the left, neither upwards nor downwards, nor through the wall. The only movement possible is to turn into one's inner self. In this experience of death, where all is abandoned and where man experiences the hopelessness of seeing no way out at all, a new dimension can emerge, a change to a life of a wholly new quality, the possibility of a leap which is neither biological nor psychological but ontological.

In philosophical language this would mean an abandoning of,

---

[12] Cf. Gertrud von Le Fort, *Die Abberufung der Jungfrau von Barby* (Munich, 1946): "I have no longer any image of God. . . . All our images have been destroyed. I saw them fall like the beautiful stars from heaven, and there is nothing left but the desert of the naked divinity" (pp. 61-2).

[13] *Op. cit.*, p. 61.

a dying to, all that is, and the touching of Being as such. Man then passes from the world that exists to Being itself, from what is created to the Ground of all creation. It seems that this experience of death is the deepest meaning of genuine religious despair today, and that it only remains sterile because it is not understood and not brought to light.

Because of the spiritual climate of our technological culture the "natural mysticism" of such an experience of death in religious despair can turn into a typically modern experience of faith: it then becomes the true experience of the cross in the life of the faith today.

If there is any truth in the scholastic axiom that "all that is, is good", then this contact with being as such must lead to a soothing peace, the discovery that despair is both poison and medicine, and that dying is a form of living. The result would be a life lived in terms of this ambivalence. And such a life would be marked, characteristically, by the almost superhuman encouraging awareness that one has left pagan fatalism far, far behind.

Can we still go further? Indeed, if this "being" became personal, a "you". This leap from Being (the God of the philosophers) to You (the God of Abraham, Isaac and Jacob, and the Father of Jesus) is still more than all previous regenerations and sudden changes an impenetrable mystery of preparation, courage, free giving, grace and freedom. For this opening up of oneself to a "you" is a matter of free decision.

The elements of a situation where this can happen can only be brought about by the presence of a helper, a "priestly" man, whose "You" bears witness to the mystery of being: the personality of God. In a personal and religious way he embodies the situation from which the call goes out, through radiation, osmosis and invitation.

Whether a man will fall in with this inducement embodied in a concrete situation and open the door for this encounter with God's "You", he must decide for himself, freely. It is a risk, a leap in the dark borne on trust, and this alone can finally overcome despair. This is hard, and far too hard for one who has never experienced a call to the "personal" life.

Looking back, we can now discern a key function for any man with a "priestly" concern, indeed a function for pastoral care in

all its aspects, whether in the form of proclamation, counselling
or celebrating the liturgy, and it is to witness through an alert
personal presence to the "You" quality of being, the personality
of God, so that the encounter with the other can become as concrete and direct as in the case of the Person of the God-Man
Jesus Christ. The art of curing the illness of despair lies in the
way one's own fully actuated person embodies the invitation to
an encounter with the Christian God.

The religious distress of today—hopelessness to the point of
despair—can only find help in the change to a personal existence.
The Christian believer must therefore recover the "lost dimension", in himself and, by radiating it, in others. The "personal
dimension" should be a sign of Christianity in the world of today,
the cure for hopelessness, and the way to the realization of the
Christian message.

*Translated by Theo Westow*

# PART II
## BULLETIN

Jean-Yves Jolif

# Joking, Irony, Hope

PART OF the success of Milan Kundera's novel, *The Joke*, with French readers was no doubt due to the fact that the French translation appeared at the end of 1968, a few months after the tragic summer in Prague.[1] In the confusion of events and feelings, *The Joke* was treated as a social document of major importance. It was thought to illustrate, elucidate and rationalize the struggles and hopes of the Czechoslovak people, and to enable a more accurate assessment to be made of the full significance of what happened on 21 August that year.

An interpretation of this sort is certainly possible. However, it is doubtful whether it is valid, because it diminishes the book's importance. It sees it as a chronicle of the years 1947–1965, or at least as history disguised as fiction, in which real events, albeit refracted through the mind of an imaginary hero, nevertheless constitute the essential content. What is forgotten, basically, is that Kundera has written a *novel*, and furthermore that this novel is possibly a great work, something quite other than a simple reflection of the society in which it was written, that on the contrary it goes beyond it and makes a deep inroad into the sensitivity of the age.[2]

The brief and tentative remarks below deliberately approach *The Joke* as a novel, that is to say (to give only a crude definition) as a search for authentic values which liberates the hero from the

[1] An English translation from a German translation, entitled *The Joke*, was published by Macdonald & Co., Ltd. (London, 1969).
[2] "Il fraye un chemin profond dans son époque": a phrase used by Louis Aragon in his preface to the French edition.

perverted world around him without, however, bringing about the radical break which alone could give access to true values.[3]

The title, *The Joke*, both suggests and conceals this search. It conceals it by appearing to indicate that the novel is wholly centred on the postcard which the young Ludvik sends a girl friend as a joke ("to hurt, shock and confuse her"), the contents of which, being anti-conformist and Trotskyist, are to have such heavy repercussions on the hero's life: exclusion from the Party and the University, consignment to a disciplinary body reserved for enemies of the regime, a scientific career compromised, resentment and desire for vengeance—right up to the week-end described in the novel when Ludvik is going to get even with the past by possessing and flouting the wife of the comrade who had voted for his exclusion. It is true that this youthful joke, together with its consequences, occupies a central position in the book: without it nothing would be left of the novel! But the title does not suggest only this joke which provides the most obvious narrative content; it provides a key to enable us gradually to perceive that there are in fact several jokes and that the novel consists in the passage from one to the other, from the most obvious to the most hidden.

We shall thus distinguish three jokes. The first is the most evident, the postcard. The third is the novel itself—not its content but its novelistic structure, in other words the fact that it is precisely a novel. By inscribing the words *"The Joke"* on the object which is the novel, Milan Kundera adopts an ironical attitude towards his work, which, according to Lukacs, is the specific attitude of the novelist to his literary creation.[4] The second joke—the intermediary between the narrative and the structure of the novel—is the one the hero discovers at the end of his search: it is useless to hope to exorcize the youthful joke by taking vengeance; a joke which was "a sorry episode, a bad joke which, not content with itself, had gone on monstrously multiplying itself into more and more stupid jokes". It is useless because it is History which is a huge joke: "Then I realized how feeble it

---

[3] For a less tentative study it is worth referring to G. Lukacs, *The Theory of the Novel*. The concepts of *problem hero, daemonic quest* and *irony* among others could be especially fruitful.

[4] *The Theory of the Novel*, notably the First Part, chapters 4 and 5.

was to want to annul my own joke, when throughout my life I was involved in a joke which was all-embracing, unfathomable and utterly irrevocable."

This is the movement in Milan Kundera's novel which we shall attempt to bring out.

The narrative begins by centring around Helena. She is the cause of Ludvik coming to spend the week-end in his home country, Moravia. In order to arrange a convenient meeting place for them both, he looks up his friend Kostka. Her time of arrival (Saturday morning, at eleven o'clock, at the station) governs what he does with his time in the hours leading up to it.[5] Since Helena, by a quirk of fate, has fallen in love with him, Ludvik is able by taking her to get at her husband, the Pavel Zemanek who had had him excluded from the Party; he goes "to ransack Pavel Zemanek's thirteenth bower; to rummage through everything and throw it about; leave everything in a shambles!" Helena lends herself only too well to this settlement of their affairs and, satisfied and happy, Ludvik savours his victory until the moment he finds out that there is nothing any longer between Helena and Pavel, that they have broken off completely and nothing has been said about it for years. Helena then emerges "stripped of everything, without a husband or any links binding her to a husband, just in *herself*", in her ugliness. By the same token, the scene immediately before, which had such profound significance for Ludvik, is now only an absurdity. More than this: the loving of Helena's naked body—the body which was to be flouted, used for revenge—seems now to flaunt a triumphal arrogance and inflicts a strange agony on Ludvik.

Ludvik's failure to be revenged, his powerlessness to recapture the past, are not solely related to the contingent fact of the break between Helena and Pavel. In a still more relentless way time deprived Ludvik's project of meaning. Quite by chance Ludvik encounters Zemanek face to face and promptly has to face reality: "He appeared to have completely abandoned his former views, and if today I had anything to do with him I would in any

[5] To be honest, other characters appear (notably Lucie and Jaroslav), but in a furtive fashion, and Ludvik does not want to meet them. Only at the end of the novel is the meaning of these ghost-like appearances made known.

conflict, like it or not, find myself taking his side. This was horrible and quite unexpected." The passing of time alone accounted for the removal of the difference which had allowed Ludvik to hate Zemanek; that which created a shocking resemblance between the former enemies was "the healing waters of time which, as we all know, can smooth over the difference between entire epochs, let alone two miserable individuals". The presence of little Brozova, Zemanek's young mistress, highlights the way time has watered everything down: "The way she and her contemporaries regarded us, we resembled each other even when we were at each other's throats", it transmutes the distant event which Ludvik still seeks to set store by into literary fiction.

In the end he has to admit it: his tryst with the past, on which he hoped to reap the harvest of revenge, is a failure for the past slips and flows by him "as phlegmatically as if it did not know me". He wants nothing better than "to disappear, isolate myself, wipe out the whole grubby devious incident, the stupid joke, wipe out Helena and Zemanek, wipe out the day before yesterday, yesterday and today, wipe it out, wipe it out so that not a trace remained". The revenge had been a fiasco; it was even more ridiculous than the joke whose consequences it was meant to annihilate. One cannot catch up with the past. To run after it is "an attempt fundamentally as useless as ashes". Time, which draws us towards the future, carries us away from the direction we are busy pursuing and gives a new meaning to all our projects.

Here is where history appears as a joke. It delivers us from desire for revenge by pointing to the vanity of it: how could Ludvik rectify his mistakes, since they were not *his*, since, all things considered, there are neither faults nor errors which could contradict the order of things, since this "order" is made up precisely of those things which human understanding takes to be exceptions and errors? But, if history is not the stern schoolmaster pointing the way towards justice and understanding among men, if history is a practical joke, then it is impenetrable and there are no longer any values. Words and gestures, poetry, music and the rites through which one attempts to perpetuate what was once rich and meaningful are no more than an unknown language. "Already for the present, history is no more than the thin thread of memory trembling above the abyss of innumerable forgotten things, but duration goes on and the time will come when individual non-elastic memories will give up when faced by dates recorded on coins long ago; whole centuries of pictures and music, centuries of discoveries, battles, books, will fall in the wake of hundreds and thousands of years, and this will be bad because man will lose his notion of himself, while his history which he can no longer conceive of or cover will shrink to a few meaningless, schematic summaries."

Finishing his lunch on the Sunday, Ludvik makes the following negative assessment: "I suddenly saw very clearly that the majority of human beings are addicted to a doubly disingenuous illusion: they believe that memory is everlasting (memory of people, things, acts, nations) and that everything is remissible (behaviour, erring ways, sins, denials of justice). Each is as false as the other. The truth is the exact reverse: everything shall be forgotten and nothing pardoned. The business of setting things to rights (through the exercise of vengeance or pardon) will belong to oblivion. No one will abolish the wrongs committed, but all wrongs will be forgotten." Ludvik is liberated from his past, but only through the loss of the world. Everything—the lime tree, the table, the people, eating, the waiter, the inn, the open door of the passage—all seem submerged in the flood of amnesia sweeping over them. The affair has come to an end, or rather it is now clear that it never existed!

There are still a few hours to go, however, before he is due to take the bus back to Prague. To get away from his obsessions, Ludvik goes out of town to wander in the open fields on the banks of the Morava. By chance he meets Jaroslav. But one can hardly call chance an unexpected meeting which so successfully calls forth and liberates a love which had been forgotten and suppressed in Ludvik, but not destroyed; a love which now swells and comes clear to tears. Jaroslav personifies his home town, youth, friendship, music, folklore, Moravia and its traditions. Without thinking, heedlessly but following the prompting of his heart, Ludvik asks his friend for permission to resume his former place in the song and dance ensemble. In a flash he rediscovers the world he had abandoned for so long, that terribly distant and remote world, which he begs to offer him sanctuary and salvation.

Why this reconciliation, which seems all of a sudden to give a positive ending to the hero's search? Why this love of the past, abruptly resurrected? Ludvik is under no illusions: if he is able to return to Moravian folklore, it is because the latter has been pushed out of the real world, because "in its misery and neglect it was abandoned by the showmen and publicists, by the political propagandists, by the purveyors of social utopias, by the swarms of cultural officials, by the rowdy—basically phoney—support of the people of my own generation, abandoned even by Zemanek; its abandonment had purified it, illuminated it with some irresistible, intimate beauty; its abandonment had given it back to me". The values which Ludvik discovers are thus values only because they are flouted, destroyed, because they cannot have a place in the real world, because they are dying. . . . A remarkable conclusion, which the final pages of the novel clarify to some extent.

Ludvik has regained his place in the ensemble which is playing in the garden of the inn. The music awakens an image in his mind, the image of Lucie—the girl he loved and lost by loving because her role as the corrupted young girl did not allow for love. He grasps how close they are to each other, even in their separation. For they were both stories of devastation. Their innocence was destroyed by an altogether vaster crime which ravaged the whole universe. The meaning of this lost love emerges: one must not bear a grudge against beautiful things which have been destroyed, one must not turn away from them resentfully, one must be full of compassion for this broken world.

The musicians continue with their concert in front of an audience enlarged by the arrival of a large crowd of youngsters and their girls—a brutal intrusion by the present, the real, which makes one want to flee, to play for oneself, to discover a protective wall in the music, "a bathyscaph weighted on to the bottom of a frozen ocean". Suddenly Jaroslav crumples up with a heart attack. The music stops. Once again, the only thing left is compassion: "Overwhelmed with grief, I gently rubbed the top of his bald head, where the sad, long hairs covered the baldness, and I realized with a shock that my trip home, made in the hope of striking at the hated Zemanek, had ended with me holding my stricken friend in my arms; yes, in that moment I could see my-self holding him in my arms, holding him and carrying him, big and heavy though he was, as if I were carrying my own mixed-up guilt, carrying him through the indifferent mob, and weeping as I went".

"One's destiny is often completed long before death, the final moment does not coincide with the moment of death": this con-clusion which Ludvik reaches is also the conclusion of the novel. The hero has torn himself away from conformism, the world no longer seems serious to him, vengeance has given way to com-passion. He is, so to speak, free. But free for what? For him there is only value in things already finished and dead even before their total disappearance, in a past doomed to oblivion; his ideal is not something to be achieved in the future, he can only be an object of compassion, one can only watch over him in the gen-eral indifference—in the same way that Jaroslav's body is being transported to the white ambulance, "through the noisy, drunken adolescents".

Ludvik's search does not, therefore, get away from abstraction. Although it brings about a break with the perverted world, it does not establish a new one in which values would be real and effec-tive; it remains fundamentally incomplete. *The Joke* is an ex-cellent illustration of the formula with which Lukacs defines the form of the novel: "The road is begun, the journey ended"; Ludvik's path reaches its end before being complete, his destiny is accomplished well before death.

That is the reason why Ludvik *is not* Milan Kundera: between author and character lies the distance created by irony. That is also why Kundera is not defined by his novel and why he cannot take it (by taking himself) completely seriously. Even more so than Ludvik's postcard, Kundera's novel is a joke! It is certainly true that the irony does not create an unbridgeable gap between the author and his hero. For the latter's search corresponds to a need in the author. Kundera would not have written his novel if in the first place it had not been a question of he himself seeking detachment from a world become congealed, in which history takes the form of destiny and which is equally incapable of pre-serving the living riches of the past and of creating a future. But it is precisely because he experiences this need that the author knows that his hero is powerless to follow his aspiration right through, to penetrate through to a world in which the values he seeks would be embodied. In placing himself at a distance from his character, in judging him, the novelist is judging himself as the author of the novel: he knows that the ideal—which by giving it the form of a novel he opposes to the real—is purely a need and not a factual reality; he knows, as Lukacs says, "the uselessness of a combat of this kind and the real's final victory". In short, an author who writes the word *joke* on his novel shows how far he has come in the direction of lucidity, of "mature virility".

Irony of this kind is neither indifference nor despair. Although the novel may be a joke, it is not thereby a tame one nor a mere practical joke like the youthful Ludvik's postcard: far from being retractable, it completely uproots society, reveals its degradation, lays bare the emptiness in all official conformism. The very fact of the novel's existence proclaims the need to invent a future; its mere presence *is* a breach in the heart of the congealed society. Although it might not *make* that future, it shows that it is both necessary and possible. It is the last or the first hope to surmount the resistance of things. One must, therefore, recognize a thin, invisible, but none the less real, continuity between the novel and political reality, *The Joke* and that Spring in Prague.

*Translated by Jonathan Cavanagh*

Lionel Blain

# Two Philosophies Centred on Hope: Those of G. Marcel and E. Bloch

## INTRODUCTION

CHARLES PÉGUY in his own inimitable way expressed astonishment at the virtue of hope. In one of his poems he has God say: Faith and love I can understand, but hope! Hope is a wonder, a miracle, a mystery, an unexpected sight in a world where the constancy of man's folly seem to undermine any basis of belief in his future improvement![1]

Following the poet's vision, theologians recently have rediscovered the mystery of hope and have been captivated by the light that emanates from its centre and which it sheds upon the whole meaning of the Christian message. But the theologians would not have succeeded in their endeavours if philosophers such as Gabriel Marcel and Ernst Bloch had not provided them with new concepts and a new language of hope. These two thinkers have riveted their attention on the experience of hope, analysed its components, described its phases and indicated its future role in man's consciousness.

In this article we shall take a brief look at these two philosophies of hope; first, that of Gabriel Marcel, the Christian neo-Socratic, who is particularly interested in the interior creativity of the act of hope and in linking its mysterious toughness to its source in the Absolute Thou; and secondly, that of Ernst Bloch, the Marxist

---

[1] *Le Porche du mystère de la deuxième vertu* (Réédition de NRF, Paris), pp. 15–23. In one section of the poem God says: "Mais l'espérance—voilà ce qui m'étonne moi-même. Ça c'est étonnant!'

theoretician, who prefers to concentrate on the possibilities in the world and to link the power of hope to the role of the future in our thinking—the Not-Yet. Thus we shall be in a position to underscore some similarities and differences between these two philosophies of hope.

## I. GABRIEL MARCEL

### *"I hope in You for us."*

It might be useful to begin by giving two definitions of hope, one stressing the relation of hope with the experience of inter-subjectivity and the other emphasizing a mysterious certainty about the Absolute as the source of hope. In the essay "On a Metaphysic of Hope" in *Homo Viator* Marcel tells us that hope is "essentially the availability of a soul which has entered intimately enough into the experience of communion to accomplish in the teeth of will and knowledge the transcendental act—the act establishing the vital regeneration of which this experience affords both the pledge and the first-fruits".[2] In another essay Marcel defines hope as that act which consists in "asserting that there is at the heart of being, beyond all data, beyond all inventories and all calculations, a mysterious principle which is in connivance with me, which cannot but will that which I will, if what I will deserves to be willed and is, in fact, willed by the whole of my being".[3]

[2] *Homo Viator, Introduction to a Metaphysic of Hope*, trans. Emma Craufurd (London: Victor Gollancz, Ltd., 1951), p. 67. (Cf. pp. 29–67.) Henceforth: HV. *Homo viator: prolégomènes à une métaphysique de l'espérance* (Paris: Aubier, 1947). Cf. (1) Marcel's *The Philosophy of Existentialism*, trans. Nanya Harari (New York: Citadel Press, 1956), pp. 9–46, "On the Ontological Mystery". Henceforth: OM. This is a translation of *Position et approches concrètes du mystère entologique* (Louvain: Nauwelaerts, 1949). (2) Marcel's *Being and Having*, trans. Katherine Farrer (New York: Harper and Row, 1965), pp. 74–92. Henceforth: BH. A translation of *Etre et Avoir* (Paris: Aubier, 1935), pp. 108–35. (3) Marcel's *The Mystery of Being, Faith and Reality*, trans. René Hague (Chicago: Henry Regnery Co., 1960), Vol. II, pp. 163–85. A translation of *Le Mystère de l'être: Foi et realité* (Paris: Aubier, 1951). (4) Marcel's *Philosophical Fragments 1909–1914*, trans. Lionel A. Blain (South Bend, Ind., U.S.A.: University of Notre Dame Press, 1965), pp. 92–102. *Fragments philosophiques 1909–1914* (Louvain: Nauwelaerts, 1962), pp. 78–92. (5) Roger Troisfontaines, *De l'existence à l'être* (Louvain: Nauwelaerts, 1953), Vol. II, pp. 173–204.    [3] OM, p. 28.

## Hope and Captivity

For Marcel, hope taken at its lowest level—where I am not concerned with important matters (like hoping for good weather) and the reasons for hoping are exterior to myself, i.e., do not have their roots "in the very depths of what I am",[4] hope is nothing but a calculation of probabilities. At its highest point of tension, however, where I take the matter to heart (like hoping for the survival of a son missing in action), hope constitutes the response of my whole being to a condition of captivity, of trial, in which I feel myself plunged. "Hope is situated within the framework of the trial, not only corresponding to it, but constituting our being's veritable *response*."[5] In hope, I long for deliverance, which would bring my trial to an end. The "I hope" aims at salvation, at "coming out of the darkness in which I am presently plunged",[6] be it illness, separation, exile, slavery, or the impossibility of "rising to a certain fullness of life, which may be in the realms of sensation or even of thought in the strict sense of the word".[7] Hope arises as a response to man's condition of captivity and alienation, be it particular or general (that is, human existence experienced as captivity).

Paradoxically, the greater my awareness of life as a confinement, the more I shall be able to experience the upsurge of hope and "to see the shining of that veiled, mysterious light, which . . . illumines the very centre of hope's dwelling place".[8] Hope is a mystery, not a problem; that is, through hope I share in the certainty which stems from participating in Being with the totality of what I am.[9]

For Marcel hope "tends inevitably to transcend the particular objects to which it at first seems to be attached".[10] The true expression of hope is not "I hope that . . ." but the absolute statement, "I hope". I may begin by hoping for some particular good, for example, a cure that I count on taking place by the end of a definite period. But as hope matures, a transformation and purification take place within me of the very notion of recovery so that if the cure does not occur, I can face the future without despair: I have acquired a new inner freedom since the very notion

[4] HV, p. 29.        [5] HV, p. 30.        [6] HV, pp. 30, 32.
[7] HV, p. 30.       [8] HV, p. 32.        [9] OM, p. 29.
[10] HV, p. 32.

of cure has been transmuted and raised to a higher level, to a
level beyond the insecurity of Having.[11]

## Source of Hope

Hope has its source in the invisible. "The estuaries of hope do
not lie entirely within the bounds of the visible world."[12] Hope is
an answer to a call, to an invitation, an answer of the creature
"to the infinite Being to whom it is conscious of owing everything that it has and upon whom it cannot impose any condition
whatever without scandal".[13] Thus hope and faith are intimately
connected. Faith in the Absolute Thou makes me look upon
despair as a kind of betrayal since faith is the "inner disposition
of one who, setting no condition or limit and abandoning himself in absolute confidence, would thus transcend all possible disappointment and would experience a security of his being...
which is contrary to the radical insecurity of Having".[14]

## Hope and Love

The fullness of hope can only be found where there is the
spiritual interconnection called love. "I hope in Thee for us" is
the best formula of hope. The nearer hope gets to charity, the
more it shares in the "unconditional quality which is the very
sign of presence" and "this presence is incarnated in the 'us' for
whom 'I hope in Thee', that is to say in a communion of which
I proclaim the indestructibility".[15] Hope and love amount to the
remedy for the temptation to self-enclosure, to a devitalization
of the self and to a systematized empiricism which is nothing but
a retraction, an inward disloyalty.[16]

## Hope, Time and Experience

For the man without hope, time is closed; the future, a vacancy,
a place of pure repetition. Hope, on the other hand, allows a man
to pierce through to a real future, to something new. That is
what Marcel means by the "prophetic character of hope".[17]

But we must not imagine that hope is a way of entering into
the secrets of God, to see what is going to happen. Still, hope

---

[11] HV, p. 46.      [12] BH, p. 77.      [13] HV, pp. 47, 63.
[14] HV, p. 46.      [15] HV, pp. 57-8, 60, 65-6.      [16] HV, p. 60.
[17] HV, p. 53.

does *affirm* as if it saw because "it draws authority from a hidden vision of which it is allowed to take account without enjoying it".[18] If time separates, hope "aims at reunion, at reconciliation: in that way . . . it might be called a memory of the future".[19]

It is in the name of a certain common-sense wisdom, of "experience", that some people oppose hope and look upon it as an illusion. Marcel wonders, however, whether this empiricism is not merely the result of a choice to remain in the dark and to avoid risk. Furthermore, hope for Marcel is rooted in what is unsullied in our being. Hope is linked "to a certain candour, a certain virginity untouched by experience".[20] One kind of experience would tell me that there is no way out of my problems or illness. Another kind of experience—and hope is at its heart—tells me that the more the real is real the less it lends itself to a calculation of possibilities on the basis of accepted experience (in the first sense of word). The person who hopes is like an inventor or a discoverer rather than like a technician; the latter never separates ends and means while the former considers the end and says that there must be a way to attain it.[21] In this sense, "in hope I do not create in the strict sense of the word, but I appeal to the existence of a certain creative power in the world, or rather to the actual resources at the disposal of this creative power".[22]

## II. Ernst Bloch

*"It is only the horizon of the future which gives reality its true dimension."*

Bloch defines hope as "the pioneer existence which we humans lead on the foremost frontier of the World-Process".[23] Man is called "to proceed beyond the horizon into that difficult degree of reality not of Being-Present (*Vorhanden-Sein*), nor of Being-in Process (*Im-Prozess-Sein*), but of Not-Yet-Being (*Noch-Nicht-Sein*), into the sphere of the Novum, of the mediation of the

[18] *Ibid.*    [19] *Ibid.*    [20] HV, p. 51.
[21] *Ibid.*    [22] HV, p. 52.
[23] "Man as Possibility", *Cross Currents*, XVIII (Summer 1968), 3, trans. William R. White, p. 280. Henceforth: MP. Cf. pp. 273–83. A translation of "De Mensch als Möglichkeit", *Forum. Oesterreichische Monat-Blätter für Kulturelle Freiheit*, XIII (1965), 140–41, pp. 357–61.

deed, of fear and hope".[24] Hope is "creative expectation".[25] To hope "belongs the knowledge that in the outside world life is as unfinished as in the Ego that works in that outside world".[26]

### Hope and Man's Future Home

For Bloch man is an incomplete being, "something which still must be found".[27] Thus the basic theme of philosophy must be man's "home which has not yet come to be, has not been achieved". "The ideal of the human essence has not yet come to be in its reality."[28] Man has an inner drive towards the future, towards a fulfilment in the future, a drive which he must take hold of and direct with courage and in risk. As a source of inspiration, Bloch says, man has the great works of art which are "a star of anticipation and a song of comfort on the way home through the darkness", as well as an "anticipatory appearance" of the utopian *novum ultimum*.[29]

### Source of Hope

For Bloch, the Marxist, there is no God; the world is sufficient for itself.[30] The primordial stuff of the universe is moved by an obscure immediate cosmic impulse, a "hunger", a tendency towards the future, towards the new. In Reality "truly new things happen. . . . Things happen which have never occurred to any man. . . . Things happen which likewise have never yet happened to any reality."[31] From the basic stuff of the universe comes the distinction between spirit and matter, i.e., the subject-object relation—a dynamic relation which tends towards a final unity. "The substratum of the real seethes on a dialectical fire. . . . The essence still has to be brought forth into the world which does not know which way is up and which therefore needs man."[32]

[24] *Ibid.*
[25] E. Bloch, *Tübinger Einleitung in die Philosophie* (Frankfurt, 1964), Vol. II, p. 176. All English translations from the works of Bloch except MP above are taken from Gerald O'Collins' *Man and His New Hopes* (New York: Herder and Herder, 1969).
[26] E. Bloch, *Das Prinzip Hoffnung* (Frankfurt, 1959), Vol. I, p. 285. Henceforth: PH.
[27] E. Bloch, *Spuren* (Frankfurt, 1959), p. 32.
[28] PH, pp. 8, 1526, 1406. Cf. pp. 1515 ff.
[29] PH, pp. 929 ff.; 247.
[30] PH, p. 1413.     [31] MP, p. 279.     [32] MP, pp. 279, 282.

As Reality divides into subject and object, spirit and matter, the drive or hunger remains in each. In man, or the subject, the hunger can become hope; in the object, possibility, i.e., the not-completely-determined. "Possibility", says Bloch, "is not hocus-pocus. It is an exactly definable concept, namely, partial conditionality. The world is not yet completely determined, is still somewhat open: like tomorrow's weather. There are conditions which we do not yet know or which do not even exist yet. . . . We live surrounded by possibility, not merely by presence. In the prison of mere 'presence we could not even move nor even breathe'."[33]

## Fluidity of Reality

One should not think of Reality as static, simple and solid. We must not let ourselves believe in the absolute immovability of "facts". Reality does not have a definitive dimension. It is not yet finished. Facts are elements in a process, elements which have been *made*, produced; but if they were produced they can also be remade, they can change, they are in flux.[34]

There is plenty of room for contingency in Reality. " 'Things can also be otherwise.' That means: things can also *become* otherwise: in the direction of evil, which would have to be avoided, or in the direction of good, which would have to be promoted."[35] We can become prisoners of "facts"—those lumps of dead matter alien to history. We can either give in to what are "evident facts" (for example, the power of an unjust economic system). But his quietism must be seen for what it is—cowardice. Or we can resist evil, evil visited from without, tenacious, obstructive evil, evil which can be eliminated by men since it was produced by men. Bloch presupposes "that the world is open, that objectively real possibilities exist in it and not merely determined necessity, not merely mechanical determinism".[36] He rejects Hegel's philosophy precisely because it does not allow for any real future, no possible surprises.[37]

## Dreams and Concreteness

Day dreams, says Bloch, may be the one thing we cannot

[33] MP, p. 281.    [34] MP, pp. 274-5.    [35] *Ibid*.
[36] PH, p. 242; MP, pp. 274, 279.    [37] MP, pp. 274, 279.
7—C.

dispense with. We need dreams if we are going to build the world of tomorrow. "So many of today's castles in the air become tomorrow's palaces, tomorrow's cities, or even tomorrow's society." [38]

The problem with dreams is that they tend to be reduced to nothingness by the obstinacy of the environment. But this is not the necessary fate of dreams. Perhaps utopias do not have to have a bad name; perhaps they do not have to turn out to be purely unrealizable ideals. But if they are to bear fruit, man must acquire a new way of seeing the world; he must be aware that something is really happening around him, and he must know what kind of conflicts are taking place in the real "so that the chasing after things in advance which have never existed, has a foot to stand on, so that it becomes concrete and mediates with the world". [39]

This means that man must "grasp something not as that which it was, not as Having-Come-into-Being, but as Coming-into-Being, a thing which has not yet played out its hand, but which seeks what belongs to it and which above all needs man in order to realize the potential pending in the World-Process". Hoping means viewing the world as a task, as a model, as an analysis of sample which is not at hand. In order for this endeavour to succeed, man needs a *docta spes*, a hope based on a speculative, metaphysical science "which not only understands the blue of the sky but even its ultra-violet", a science bringing an awareness "that the presence which is usually called reality is surrounded by a tremendously greater ocean of objectively real possibility". [40]

## Appearance of the Not-Yet

According to Bloch, the Not-Yet-Being appears both as the not-yet-come-into-being and as the not-yet-conscious (the creatively pre-conscious). Hopefully the not-yet-conscious is an expression of what is not yet but is coming; it represents the not-yet-come-into-being.

The not-yet-conscious can sometimes be identified as the no-longer-conscious "down there in the cellar of consciousness where what was once conscious has sunken low, where it decays or is summoned up again".

[38] MP, p. 273.                    [39] MP, pp. 274, 279.
[40] MP, pp. 280–81; *Verfremdungen* (Frankfurt, 1962), Vol. I, p. 219.

Bloch asserts that the not-yet-conscious can be visible without being in circulation on the level of consciousness. The not-yet-conscious shows itself more clearly, makes its presence felt more surely under one set of conditions than under another set. The "hunger" in the spirit appears as most active when the conditions exist in which the percentage of the not-yet-conscious is the greatest: in youth, in changing times and in productivity. In these circumstances, hope bursts forth most strikingly; the future, the Not-Yet, enters into the fluid present and though it is not completely delineated it has enough consistency to give a whole new thrust to life. Utopias, dreams and revolutionary ideals make their appearance. And a process of transformation is begun because of them.[41]

But nothing is fully predetermined. Man is needed. "Man makes the decision for something undecided." The moving reality outside needs man to guide it in the direction of the good. There is something for man to do. He needs the courage to accept the challenge of hope and the inevitable risk involved in building the future. *"Natura naturans* ... meets man half-way and gives him a well-founded direction so that he can act creatively in a concrete manner and in complete seriousness—not with confidence, for that would be based upon a determined world, but with fear and hope which are based on the not-yet-determined."[42]

## CONCLUSION

The two philosophies of hope here analysed have some interesting similarities, while differing on some very basic points. Both stress the notion that man is on a pilgrimage, Marcel pointing to the condition of captivity as a correlate of hope while Bloch sees man looking ahead to the time when his true home has been built, when the ideal of man's essence has been realized. Both criticize the attitude of capitulation before what are considered obstinate "facts" or "experience"; and they stress the fluidity of these facts (Bloch) and the higher form of experience which opens new horizons for man (Marcel). According to both

[41] MP, p. 281; PH, pp. 16, 1404, 1417.
[42] MP, pp. 282–3.

philosophers, hope initiates a creative process, or rather it taps the resources already present and at work in the real—God for Marcel and Dialectical Reality for Bloch—and shows us the future without letting us in on the secrets of God or of Reality. Both authors are conscious of the risk of hope, Bloch emphasizing that fear must be faced with courage while Marcel maintains that the function of hope is to overcome the temptation to affirm the ultimate bankruptcy of life and reality. Both underscore the social and intersubjective side of hope, Marcel saying that the experience of communion in love is the door to hope while Bloch sees the future being built by a whole class of men sharing the same ideals and heading towards the achievement of a classless society. Marcel visualizes the consummation of hope on the other side of death in the supernatural unity of a multitude of men united in a kingdom of love under the Absolute Thou. He does not exclude the need for actively participating in the building of a better world, of an earthly future. Hope that is inactive is an illusion. But his whole philosophy is suffused with the idea that the death of the beloved constitutes a test of presence and fidelity which will come to an end in the Presence of the Absolute Thou. Bloch's perspective on the other hand is uncompromisingly naturalistic. He thrills at the certainty that newness bursts forth in Reality both in the subject and in the object. However, the individual's whole satisfaction and consolation resides in the projected realization of man's essence—the classless society.

Ferdinand Kerstiens

# The Theology of Hope
# in Germany Today

## I. The Problem

AT THE beginning of this century Charles Péguy wrote in the introduction to his book *The Key to the Mystery of Hope*: "The faith I love best, says God, is hope". Only today has theology caught up with the prophetic content of this terse message and begun to understand it. In the last decade hope has become a central theme of theology, almost to the point of being fashionable. The publications concerned with this theme are legion.

The impulse did not come from theology itself, but from a basic change in the patterns of thought and experience that express our present understanding of reality. At least since Karl Marx wrote in his 11th thesis on Feuerbach: "The philosophers have only given different interpretations of reality. The question is to change it", it has become obvious that the world, including the social environment, is no longer seen as a fixed framework into which human life has to be fitted, but rather as the raw material with which to build a better future, as a matter of change, not of conformity.

At the same time the development of science and technology as well as the start made with industrialization have opened up ways in which this task can be tackled. This new outlook on the future and the search for an orientation have found expression in numerous collections of the most varied kinds of studies and the most diverse approaches to the problems of progress, the future and hope.[1]

[1] E. Burck (ed.), *Die Idee des Fortschritts* (Munich, 1963); H. Kühn and

Traditional Catholic theology understood hope mainly as something that would lead us out of this world and its history towards total fulfilment with God.[2] Evangelical dialectic theology understood eschatological faith as a turning away from this world. Neither could cope with the new awareness and the modern mentality. With regard to these new problems both rather gave the impression of being escapist.

The new reflection on hope is the belated answer of theology to this change in awareness. In what follows I shall not attempt an analysis of this development, but rather a methodical presentation of the present *status questionis* in the theology of hope.[3]

## II. THE THEOLOGY OF HOPE IN THE OLD TESTAMENT

### 1. *The Tradition of Prophetic History*

An analysis of a theology of hope can well begin with the experience of Yahweh in the Old Testament.[4] Yahweh is the God of the deliverance from Egypt, the God of the nomads, who leads his people into a new country. For all this, he does not surrender himself to his people; he cannot be forced by magic; he shows himself to his people as always near but beyond any kind of manipulation, as the one who is always more powerful, yet not overwhelming.[5]

---

F. Weidemann, *Die Philosophie und die Frage nach dem Fortschritt* (Munich, 1964); *Die Hoffnungen unserer Zeit. Zehn Beiträge* (Munich, 1964); U. Schöndorfer (ed.), *Der Fortschrittsglaube, Sinn und Gefahren* (Graz, 1965); *Säkularisation und Utopie. Ebracher Studien. Festschr. E. Forsthoff* (Stuttgart, 1967); G. Walstenholme (ed.), *Man and his Future* (a symposium of twenty-seven scientists on the elements of a biological revolution; a Ciba Foundation volume, London, 1963).

[2] The many treatises on eschatology are silent on this point until M. Schmaus, *Katholische Dogmatik* IV, 2 (5th ed., Munich, 1959).

[3] Two surveys of work done on this point by Catholic theologians have been used here (henceforth referred to by their authors' names): G. Greshake, *Auferstehung der Toten. Ein Beitrag zur gegenwärtigen theologischen Diskussion über Zukunft und Geschichte* (Essen, 1969) and F. Kerstiens, *Hoffnungsstruktur des Glaubens* (Mainz, 1969).

[4] H. D. Preuss, *Jahweglaube und Zukunfteserwartung*. Beitr. z. Wiss. v. A. u.N.T., Heft 7, with extensive bibliography (Stuttgart, 1968); V. Maag, "Malkut JHWH," in *VT*. Suppl. VII (1960), pp. 129–53; Greshake, pp. 173–208; Kerstiens, pp. 95–112.

[5] For the analysis of the name of God, see T. C. Vriezen, "Ehje aser ehje", in *Festschrift f. A. Bertholet* (Tübingen, 1950), pp. 498–512; G. von Rad,

He points to the future, to his future dealings with man, and in this process he is recognized if man clings to him in faith. Every fulfilment experienced bears within it for Israel a new and greater promise, so that Israel is gradually driven into an expanding future.

In all this the promise itself leaves room for decision, room for rejection and defection to false gods, but also for conversion and faithfulness.

Yahweh is therefore not the guarantor of the existing order, of the cosmos, of a temporal perfect origin like a golden age, to which man returns in mythical cycles. He is rather the God that dominates history,[6] who invites his people to change the world on the lines indicated by his promises, constantly to leave the existing order in order to shape the future in response to this divine invitation.

Israel therefore understood history as something dynamic and active, something that derived its sense of direction from the saving deeds of Yahweh.[7] And so the hope of Israel is centred in a concrete way on the future of this world, which dawns on the horizon.[8]

Israel's experience, with its reference back to past deeds of

---

*Theologie des Alten Testaments* I (4th ed., Munich, 1962), pp. 193-9; and the commentaries on Ex. 3. 14, esp. that of M. Noth, *Das Zweite Buch Moses*. ATD vol. 5 (Göttingen, 1961), pp. 30 f.

[6] Israel's understanding of the theology of creation can only be understood in the context of promise and future. It arose in the wake of the universalization of the "covenant-God", and his recognition as Lord over all other gods and nations. See G. von Rad, *Theologie des A.T.* I, pp. 149-67; *id.*, "Theologische Probleme des alttestamentlichen Schöpfungsglaubens", in his *Ges. Studien zum A.T.* (Munich, 1958), pp. 136-47; R. Rendtorff, "Die theologische Stellung des Schöpfungsglaubens von Deuterojesaja", in *Zeitschr. f. Theol. u. Kirche* 51 (1964), pp. 3-1S3.

[7] A. Weiser, *Glaube und Geschichte im Alten Testament* (Göttingen, 1961), pp. 99-182; G. von Rad, *Theologie des AT* I and II (vol. II, 3rd ed., Munich, 1962); C. Westermann (ed.), *Probleme alttestamentlicher Hermeneutik* (Munich, 1961); W. Zimmerli, *Gottes Offenbarung* (Munich, 1963); R. Rendtorff, "Die Offenbarungsvorstellungen im alten Israel", in W. Pannenberg (ed.), *Offenbarung als Geschichte*. Kerygma u. Dogma, Beiheftl (2nd ed.; Göttingen, 1963).

[8] H. Eising, "Die Berufung Israels: Sinn und Erfüllung", in W. Heinen and J. Schreiner (ed.), *Erwartung–Verheissung–Erfüllung* (Würzburg, 1969), pp. 33-62; J. Schreiner, "Was verheissen Israels Propheten?" in *op. cit.*, pp. 86-110.

Yahweh in the history of his people, its reference forward contained in the promises, and the aims embodied in his people's mission—all this enables man to think in terms of a much wider historical framework because he is involved in the covenant as a partner.

This perspective of hope arouses the forces man needs to master the future of this world in faithfulness to Yahweh. It allows man to give meaning to the past by the recognition of the fulfilment of past promises and of judgments that have come true, and both these factors point to the opportunity to build and expect a still greater future through a radical response to God. Most biblical scholars agree on this interpretation of the way Israel understood history.

## 2. The Controversy about the Apocalyptic Writings

One of the great achievements of Israel is that it did not allow this hope to vanish during the period of the exile and after. During this time the message of hope found expression in apocalyptic writings, partly derived from sources outside Israel. And in the interpretation of this apocalyptic trend the scholars are at loggerheads with each other.[9] What is the controversy about?

For some the apocalyptic view condemns man to total passivity. Whatever man does happens in this aeon which will disappear

[9] J. M. Schmidt, *Die jüdische Apokalyptik*. Die Geschichte ihrer Erforschung von den Anfängen bis zu den Textfunden von Qumran (Neukirchen, 1969); J. Schreiner, *Alttestamentlich-jüdische Apokalyptik*. Eine Einführung (Munich, 1969); Greshake, pp. 219–33; Kerstiens, pp. 112–9. For the *negative* criticism see G. von Rad, *Theologie des AT* II, pp. 314–21; G. Fohrer, "Die Struktur alttestamentlicher Eschatologie", in *Theol. Lit. Zeitschr.* 85 (1960), pp. 401–20; A. Oepke, "Kalypto", art. in *Theol. Wörterbuch z. NT* III, p. 581; G. Sauter, *Zukunft und Verheissung*. Das Problem der Zukunft in der gegenwärtigen theologischen und philosophischen Diskussion (Zurich, 1965), pp. 229–51. For the *positive* criticism, see H. Gross, "Die Entwicklung alttestamentlicher Heilshoffnung", in *Trierer Theol. Zeitschr.* 70 (1961), pp. 15–28; M. Noth, *Das Geschichtsverständnis der alttestamentlichen Apokalyptik* (Cologne, 1954); K. Koch, "Spät-israelitisches Geschichtsdenken am Beispiel des Buches Daniel", in *Hist. Zeitschr.* 193 (1961), pp. 1–32; A. Strobel, *Kerygma und Apokalyptik* (Göttingen, 1967); E. Käsemann, "Zum Thema urchristlicher Apokalyptik", in his *Exegetische Versuche und Besinnungen* (2nd ed., Göttingen, 1965), pp. 105–31; W. Pannenberg, "Dogmatische Thesen", in *Offenbarung als Geschichte* (see n. 7), pp. 91–114; J. Moltmann, *Theologie der Hoffnung* (6th ed., Munich, 1966), pp. 120–4 (London ed., *Theology of Hope*, 1968).

completely and must even be destroyed in order to make room for the new aeon which already exists with God and only waits to be revealed. This is a betrayal of the prophetic view of history which made man co-responsible for history and its future, and which is here abandoned in favour of an esoteric teaching that claims to see through this end of the world which God has determined already.

Others see it as an attempt to see history as a whole in the light of God's plan where everything has its once-for-all place and value. In this view the image of history expands from the Yahwist to the apocalyptic writer. Instead of seeing only particular events the events and issues are seen in a constantly wider context as divine revelation. Man sees God at work in his dealings with Israel and all other nations till in the end the whole cosmos is understood in its total history as the revelation of Yahweh. This contains a message for the future and arouses a hope which, though patient, is not passive, and creates an endurance, an active faithfulness to God, that does not succumb to extreme distress, even in historic failures. And this leads to an understanding of Jesus' cross and resurrection.

This controversy is still going on. But the growing number of publications connected with it shows the importance of this topic in the new problem of the relations between hope, history and the world.

### III. The Theology of Hope in the New Testament

The problem of the immediate expectation and delay of the parousia, and that of an eschatology of the present or of the future, have preoccupied scholars for many years.

Old Testament hermeneutics, research in the ways the Semites felt and thought, and the theological study of hope and future as understood by the modern mind, have brought new life to the exegesis of the New Testament. Here we can only deal with the theology of Christ's resurrection and the theology of hope which flows from it.[10]

[10] F. Mussner, *Die Auferstehung Jesu* (Munich, 1969, with ext. bibl.); P. Hoffmann, *Die Toten in Christus.* Neutest. Abh., Neue Folge, vol. 2 (Münster, 1966); K. Lehmann, *Auferweckt am dritten Tage nach der Schrift.* Quaest.

The resurrection of Jesus has for long played only a secondary role in Catholic theology as an apologetic proof of the divinity of Christ. This use of the Easter message has yielded to the pressure of more careful scholarship in hermeneutics, and this has again brought to light the importance of Jesus' resurrection for the whole of theology.

The Easter message is now understood as prophecy at its highest possible level in this aeon. It is seen as the concrete fulfilment of the promise of a future which is already inaugurated in the new life of the believer and anticipates its realization.[11]

This anticipation of the promised future has broken through the apocalyptic interpretation of the resurrection. But this means that even for Christ everything has not yet happened. As risen, he still has a new future in front of him, namely, the drawing of all men and the world into his resurrection.

The "eschatological difference" between the resurrection of Jesus and that of the dead now throws open the new meaning of history where there is scope for responsibility and rejection, for a mission and a new shaping of the world in terms of that promised future which has already started.

This has drawn eschatology out of its isolation at the end of dogmatic theology and has created a new understanding of the fact that the eschatological dimension affects the whole of a Christian's existence. Consequently, the whole of Christian theology becomes, in all its branches, "the science of this striving of the resurrection towards the future of Christ".[12]

Today the discussion concentrates on three points; the character of the resurrection of Jesus as an event, the way the disciples experienced the Easter event, and the meaning of the Easter message for the future.

---

disp. 38 (Freiburg, 1968); J. Moltmann, *op. cit.*, pp. 125–209; *id., Perspektiven der Theologie*, Gesammelte Aufsätze (Munich/Mainz, 1968); W. Pannenberg, *Grundzüge der Christologie* (Gütersloh, 1964); *id.* (ed.), *Offenbarung als Geschichte* (see n. 7); Greshake, pp. 239–304; Kerstiens, pp. 123–8.
[11] K. Kertelge, *"Rechtfertigung" bein Paulus*. Neutest. Abh., N.F., vol. 3 (Münster, 1967); P. Stuhlmacher, *Gerechtigkeit Gottes bei Paulus* (Göttingen, 1965); U. Lutz, *Das Geschichtsverständnis des Paulus*. Beitr. zur Ev. Theol., vol. 49 (Munich, 1968); W. Dantine, "Rechtfertigung und Gottesgerechtigkeit", in *Verkündigung und Forschung*, Beih. zur "Ev. Theol." Heft 2 (1966), pp. 68–100.        [12] J. Moltmann, *op. cit.*, p. 177.

The reception of the Easter message happens in this way: man inserts himself into this new historical orientation opened up by Christ's resurrection; he does so through a faith which is at the same time a hope of fulfilment, and by striving towards the change of this world through the practice of a Christian life. This hope is not an addition, an afterthought, to faith, but the very heart of faith itself.[13]

## IV. SOME FURTHER CONSIDERATIONS

Apart from the achievements in biblical scholarship, and linked with them, the debate provoked by the work of Teilhard de Chardin[14] and Ernst Bloch[15] became important for theology. The dialogue between the *Paulusgesellschaft* and the Marxists also brought greater depth to the theological discussion about the meaning of the Christian message for the future and as loaded with historical initiative.[16]

The dialogue with critical social theory, philosophical hermeneutics and scientific futurology is typical of this new theology

[13] O. Kuss, *Der Römerbrief* (Regensburg, 1957), pp. 195–8; H. Schlier, "Uber die Hoffnung", in his *Besinnung auf das NT* (2nd ed., Freiburg, 1967), pp. 135–45; N. Brox, *Die Hoffnung des Christen* (Vienna, 1965); E. Käsemann, *Paulinische Perspektiven* (Tübingen, 1969); W. Thüsing, "Der Gott der Hoffnung (Rom. 15. 13)", in W. Heinen and J. Scheiner, *op. cit.*, pp. 63–85.

[14] For the theological significance of Teilhard de Chardin, see G. Crespy, *Das theologische Denken Teilhard de Chardins* (Stuttgart, 1963).

[15] For the theological significance of E. Bloch, see S. Unseld (ed.), *Ernst Bloch zu ehren*. Beiträge zu seinem Werk (Frankfurt, 1965), esp. the contributions by Metz, Moltmann and Pannenberg; E. Kimmerle, *Die Zukunftsbedeutung der Hoffnung*. Auseinandersetzung mit dem Hauptwerk Ernst Blochs (Bonn, 1966); W. D. Marsch, *Hoffen worauf?* Eine Auseinandersetzung mit Ernst Bloch (Hamburg, 1963); G. Sauter, *op. cit.*, pp. 277–348.

[16] K. Rahner, R. Garaudy and J. B. Metz, *Der Dialog oder Ändert sich das Verhältnis zwischen Katholizismus und Marxismus* (Hamburg, 1966); *Schöpfertum und Freiheit. Dokumente der Paulusgesellschaft* 19 (Munich, 1968); K. Rahner, "Über die theologische Problematik der 'Neuen Erde'," in his *Schriften zur Theologie* VIII (Einsiedeln, 1967), pp. 580–92; *id.*, "Immanente und transzendente Vollendung der Welt", *ibid.*, pp. 593–612; *id.*, "Marxistische Utopie und christliche Zukunft des Menschen", in his *Schriften zur Theologie* VI (Einsiedeln, 1965), pp. 77–90; G. Sauter, "The Future: A Question for the Christian-Marxist Dialogue", in *Concilium* (Jan. 1969), pp. 63–7 (American edn., vol. 41).

of hope. As a result of all this, theology is again in contact with the cultural and political trends of today.[17]

The lines pursued by this new theology often cross each other and also those of non-theological projects. The terminology is still so fluid that it has given rise to much misunderstanding and phoney controversies, so that we can only refer here to some results of the discussion.

1. J. Moltmann's *Theology of Hope* has provoked widespread discussion.[18] The emphatic agreement and determined criticism of Moltmann's approach show that he touched a vulnerable spot in our theology, a gap in the relationship between theology, the awareness of faith and responsibility for the world. Moltmann stresses the practical implications of a hope which is rooted in the resurrection of Jesus, and, because of this, demands that the community be constantly involved in a new exodus from the "establishment" in any form.

This theological interpretation breaks out of the narrow view which sees the message of the resurrection as an (untenable) historical report or as a mere call for decision. On the contrary, it sees the resurrection as an opening up of the historical process and as a promise in response to which the Christian is compelled to be committed to change in an effective way.

This frees the Church from the popular view that it is merely a reservoir for social drop-outs, and turns it into the spearhead of mankind's future and a thorn in the flesh of present establishments. The freedom, given by Christ and experienced as coming from Christ, the message of the Kingdom of God, do not merely mean inner freedom and bliss, but also, and by the same token,

---

[17] G. Sauter, *op. cit.*; J. Pieper, *Hoffnung und Geschichte* (Munich, 1967); W. D. Marsch, *Zukunft* (Stuttgart, 1969); W. Heinen and J. Schreiner, *op. cit.*; E. Schillebeeckx, *Gott und die Zukunft des Menschen* (Mainz, 1969); Greshake, pp. 321–411; Kerstiens, pp. 189–226.

[18] Cf. J. Moltmann, the works already mentioned; W. D. Marsch (ed.), *Diskussion über die "Theologie der Hoffnung"* (Munich, 1967, with ext. bibl.); W. Kreck, *Die Zukunft des Gekommenen*. Grundprobleme der Eschatologie (2nd ed., Munich, 1966); P. Schütz, *Freiheit–Hoffnung–Prophetie*. Von der Gegenwärtigkeit des Zukünftigen. Ges. Werke III (Hamburg, 1963). It should be mentioned that Schütz's previous work in the direction of a new theology of hope was on many points taken up by Moltmann and others without any reference to him. Kerstiens, pp. 120–57.

*shalom* (positive peace) for man as a whole, in his social relationships, peace on earth and deliverance from transitoriness.

God is then not the "wholly other" but rather the one that changes all. This is possible because the future in Christ has already impressed a sense of direction on the past and thus stresses the importance of the present.

The discussion about the theology of hope here concentrates on the following three points: whether Moltmann does not see salvation too much in the future and so underrates the new life already given in justification; how imperatives for action can be derived from promises, and what the relation is between the future of this world and the future that is promised.

2. J. B. Metz's "political theology"[19] brings out a double concern. It seeks to be a discerning correction of all the transcendental, existential and personalist interpretations of Jesus' message, and to overcome the gap, created in the period of the Enlightenment, between religion and society by an individualistic interpretation of the Christian message and faith. On the other hand, it constitutes an attempt to apply Christ's eschatological universalist message to the conditions of modern society, its structures and public life, its problems and opportunities.

This transmission of Christ's message cannot remain purely theoretical but must prove and justify itself in practice. The eschatological message itself is the source of permanent public criticism of any "established present", revealing its need for constant change and inspiring new initiatives for further humanization.

But this transmission of the criticism implied in Christ's message can only be provided by a Church that can criticize its own practice ideologically, a Church that is fully aware of the gap between its own reality and the message, and genuinely tries to bridge this gap.[20]

The debate concerns the problems whether this approach does not reduce the message of Christ to a political initiative by making

[19] J. B. Metz, *Zur Theologie der Welt* (Mainz/Munich, 1968), pp. 99–146; *id.*, "Politische Theologie", in *Sacramentum Mundi* III; H. Peukert (ed.), *Diskussion zur "Politischen Theologie"* (Mainz-Munich, 1969, with ext. bibl.).

[20] J. B. Metz, *Reform und Gegenreformation heute* (Mainz-Munich, 1969).

theology indulge in politics, and whether in any case the Church has the ability and the mission to act as an agent of social criticism,

3. The basis of R. Shaull's "theology of revolution"[21] differs from that of the political theology we have just mentioned. It sprang mainly from an analysis of the Church's social situation and its social responsibility for a more human world. From the point of view of experience it has been prompted above all by the situation in Latin America where, according to many, revolution is the only solution.

God's dealings with man are aimed at making man change the world. The coming of Christ and the work of his Spirit have introduced new disturbing factors into history. The Christian only experiences this kind of God when he inserts himself into this movement and puts his shoulder to the wheel of revolution. The political revolutionary terminology then serves to provide a secular explanation of the coming of the Kingdom of God.

The difficulty in the explanation of this theology of revolution lies above all in the confused concept of revolution. Every author has his own version. A further difficulty lies in the (necessary) mixing of theology with sociological, economic, political and psychological data and theories. Particularly the problem of violence in the revolutionary process is far from having been solved.

4. A new spiritual theology of hope is beginning to emerge. From its beginning this theology of hope was never a merely academic issue but always implied the question of how to live Christianity in practice.[22]

Christian hope is not opposed to the hopes of this world. All these hopes are rather the means through which the one hope is

[21] E. Feil and R. Weth (ed.), *Diskussion zur "Theologie der Revolution"* (Mainz/Munich, 1969, with documents and ext. bibl.); R. Rendtorff and H. E. Tödt, *Theologie der Revolution, Analysen und Materialien* (ed. Suhrkamp 258, 2nd ed., Frankfurt, 1966); Harvey Cox, *The Secular City* (2nd ed., New York, 1966); *id., God's Revolution and Man's Responsibility* (Valley Forge).

[22] See esp. L. Boros, *Erlöstes Leben* (Mainz, 1965); *id., Im Menschen Gott begegnen* (Mainz, 1967); *id., Aus der Hoffnung leben.* Zukunftserwartung in christlichem Denken (Olten, 1968); J. Moussé, *L'Espérance des Hommes* (Paris, 1968); A. Grabner, *In Gottes Zukunft.* Theol. Med., Heft 22 (Einsiedeln, 1968); K. Rahner, "Die Zukunft der Kirche hat schon begonnen", in *Handbuch der Pastoraltheologie* IV (Freiburg, 1969), pp. 744–59; cf. also the various relevant contributions in this issue of *Concilium*.

mediated. Man meets God's future by facing his worldly future. Here Christian hope co-ordinates, criticizes and gathers together the hopes of this world, rises above them, and fulfils them when they reach their limit.

Thus Christian hope inspires the Christian commitment to the neighbour at the individual as at the social level, right up to the laying down of one's own life and possible failure in this world, because death itself cannot break down this hope. For Christian hope is born of, and derives its efficacy from, Christ's death and victory over death, his resurrection.

In this perspective of hope the Christian can accept his encounters with other men, the humdrum life of every day, the frequent moments of resignation and the many frustrations of modern society, the darkness of the hidden nearness of God and the imperfection of his Church. There he will also understand his true mission.

Even after death hope will not simply pass into fulfilment. It will "remain" (I Cor. 13.13) as surrender in trust and wonder to a God who proves himself always greater and to the free flow of his love. It remains as a readiness to accept God himself as the eternal and inexhaustible gift of his love.[23]

[23] K. Rahner, "Zur Theologie der Hoffnung", in his *Schriften zur Theologie* VIII, pp. 561–79; L. Boros, *Erlöstes Leben*, pp. 28 f; Kerstiens, pp. 210–14.

*Translated by Theo Westow*

Jan Peters

# Black Theology as a Sign of Hope

THIS ISSUE of *Concilium* is devoted to the question of spirituality. Its aim will be to show that what we affirm and profess as believers has an existential reference. If the Christian asserts that he has been redeemed and claims that a new kind of life is residing in him—a life that is a source of liberating energy—then these convictions must acquire an existential form and aspect expressed in his mode of living. Otherwise they will degenerate into an ideology that seeks merely to legitimate life as a *de facto* reality; and they will fail to manifest themselves in any authentic manner as a *source* of life. The Christian must therefore be the very opposite of what Nietzsche remarked of him: that the Christian gives not the faintest sign of having been redeemed. To put it in scriptural terms: the Christian cannot behave like those who have no hope.

The venture represented by Vatican II is through and through that kind of living out of hope. The fact that at a juncture when the Faith has lost everything of its self-evidencing character and has almost ceased to be given either incentive or affirmation from outside, the Catholic community has dared to grapple with the prospects for belief, without invoking in advance what spiritual powers that action may invoke, is—taken by and large—a sign of hope. One can say, of course, in retrospect that for many—including some, even, of those who had originally set the process in motion—that hope has been dashed. But then this applies primarily to those who confuse such hope with a superficial optimism or with what Ricoeur calls *"le prospectif"*, foresight, in the sense of the adage: management is foresight: sizing up the future rationally and making it economically feasible—but without the extra risk involved when we venture to leap into the gap bored by an outlook, a vista (*le perspectif*) in the mists of uncertainty. Of course the care and the technical mode of action entailed by foresight (*prospectif*) do constitute a kind of secular hope; it must even be present, if there is to be any justification for a form of hope both more subtle and more hazardous.

There is a hope in the short term and a hope in the long term. The former is warranted and upborne by the degree of rational insight and understanding, of *"logos"* (cf. futuro*logy*), of probability, of calculated chance, of reduced risk. That is why the short-term variety of hope calls for less moral courage, less of the resolve needed for taking the plunge into the gap presented by the future; and why the man thus furnished with a secular mode of hoping stands less chance of losing his vision. Hope in the longer term presupposes an unshakable faith, an awareness of the risks and a readiness to allow, on an existential basis, for the possibility that outwardly the vision may be lost. Yet it sharpens that faculty of vision which tradition knows as "the eye of faith".

When we speak here of Black Theology as a sign of hope, "hope" is to be understood as hope in the long term. We do not mean by "hope" a superficial optimism that starts exulting as soon as the first swallow of the theological spring makes its appearance. By "hope" in this instance we most emphatically mean hope of the long-term variety, hope which responds to a vista, a "perspective", of its own creation, a long-term hope running deliberate risks that vision may be lost. The justification for such a kind of hope (for even this hope that is in us needs justifying— 1 Peter 3. 15) lies precisely in the perspective that is opened up.[1] A great deal, therefore, will depend on whether in this article we can succeed in making such a perspective visible in the complex whole denoted by the term "Black Theology". With that in view it would seem useful to start by taking a closer look at the phenomenon of Black Theology[2] in its social context. Only then

---

[1] For Ricoeur's distinction between *"le perspectif"* and *"le prospectif"*, cf. his "Prévision économique et choix éthique", in *Histoire et vérité* (Paris, 1967³), pp. 301–16.

[2] As a source of ready information cf. Charles Gafer, *White reflections*

8—C.

will it become clear whether this phenomenon really does afford
a broadened, amplified perspective when one sets it alongside the
pattern of expectation provided by the Christian hope: the coming
(*adventus*) of His Kingdom. Thus we are not concerned with
pointing to the hope which resides in individuals like Martin
Luther King, Abernathy or Jackson, but with interpreting a collective event in the world of coloured people as giving grounds
for hope in the future of Christianity. Let it be said straightaway
that the phenomenon of Black Theology is in part explicable in
terms of political, economic, juridical, psychological and racial
factors. It is impossible in this article to do more than indicate
the motive and purpose of Black Theology as seen from the stand-
point of these several areas of knowledge.[3] They are to be regarded not as excluding a theological motivation, but rather as

on *Black Power* (Grand Rapids, 1970) and Sterling Tucker, *Black reflections on White Power* (Grand Rapids, 1970). For a deeper analysis of the
background and ideology, Nathan Wright, Jr., *Black Power and Urban
Unrest* (New York, 1967); Stokely Carmichael and Charles V. Hamilton,
*Black Power: The Politics of Liberation in America* (New York, 1967);
Vincent Harding, "The Religion of Black Power", in D. Cutler (ed.),
*The Religious Situation 1968* (Boston, 1968). Black Theology proper is no
more than two years old; prominent theologians are, e.g., Archie Har-
graves of the Chicago Theological Seminary and Thomas Ogletree of the
Lutheran School of Theology, besides Charles Wesley and Eric Lincoln
of the Union Theological Seminary in New York, which registered an
immediate reaction to the so-called Black Manifesto. With noticeably less
resonance this problem has also been broached in Africa: V. Mulago, "Le
problème d'une Théologie Africaine revu à la lumière de Vatican II", in
*Revue du Clergé Africain*, 24, nos. 3–4 (May/July 1969), pp. 277–314, and,
with very great reservations on behalf of a universal theology: A. Vanneste,
"Théologie universelle et théologie africaine", in *ibid.*, pp. 324–36; Horst
Bürkle, *Theologie und Kirche in Afrika* (Stuttgart, 1968). Very instruc-
tive in this context is the account of the emergence of a small, independent Christian church in the Yoruba country: H. W. Turner, *African In-
dependent Church* (London, 1967), with detailed bibliography. See also,
"Die Zweite Allafrikanische Kirchenkonferenz", in *Herder Korrespondenz*
(October 1969), pp. 455–7.
[3] Cf., e.g., Otto Klineberg, *Characteristics of the American Negro* (New
York, 1944); Gunnar Myrdal, *An American Dilemma. The Negro Problem and Modern Democracy*, vol. 1 (New York, 1944); Julius Horwitz,
*The W.A.S.P.* (New York, 1967) (W.A.S.P. being an abbreviation of
White Anglo-Saxon Protestant); E. Digby Baltzell, *The Protestant Establishment. Aristocracy and Caste in America* (New York, 1964). It is typical
that most of the books on "black problems" come from white authors. Of
the total book production in 1969 (22,000 new titles) only 35 titles were by

forming a challenge to theology not to lose sight of this phenomenon or steer clear of it altogether.

## I. The "Black Theology" Phenomenon in an Adventual Perspective

We employ the unaccustomed term "adventual"[4] here in order
to intimate that we have in mind not a futuristic or even futuro-
logical perspective, but the perspective acquired when with the
"eye of faith" we look towards the *adventus Domini* as a so far
unfulfilled event in salvation history. The distinction maintained
here between *adventus* and *futurum*, between someone who is
coming in our direction and "what is to come", namely, the
future, might appear to be a rarified one. Yet it suggests at any
rate two different planes. What man *qua* historical being finds
himself confronted with as "future" is always uncertain and for
that reason menacing. This margin of threat man himself can
narrow down, through the advance of systematic knowledge in
its various branches, by introducing "logos", a degree of insight
and comprehension, into that future here and now. Christian conviction, however, also apprehends that future as a God who is
coming towards us in person. In Jesus of Nazareth this—the fact
that a personal God comes in our direction—has become an historical reality which is not as yet completed: God is he who is
still coming. He is not only the One who has already revealed
himself; he is at the same time the One who continues to reveal
himself, who never lapses into absolute silence. Because of this
conviction the future is not just matter for thought; it is also
matter for hope, in the Christian sense: the future is not purely
impersonal, not an anonymous entity "over against" man; it too
has a "face"—the face and aspect of One who is personally well
disposed towards human beings, of One who comes towards us
and whom we are to expect: *adventus Domini*.

Another contribution to this number, *à propos* of negro
spirituals, characterizes the Christianity of black people as the
living embodiment of an abridged, truncated Gospel. This is

---

black authors. The promotion of a university study course especially for
blacks is resulting in a slight increase in the negligible number of black
bookshops.

bound up with the social predicament of blacks in the United States (their servile existence) and their constricted consciousness. For a time, the only function of Christianity was to bring some light into what was for them the *status quo*: their exclusion from the life of the whites, an apprehension of their a-social situation as a cross, a way of suffering, as an identification with the Suffering Servant of Isaiah, the ever journeying and ever wandering People of Israel, with the suffering Christ or—a telling symptom of their sense of inferiority—with Simon of Cyrene.

One can try to uncover the reasons why the blacks' Christianity has picked and chosen from the Scriptures; but then one will be brought face to face, not with racial divergences but with a set of social malcircumstances. Outside the United States, for instance, in those countries of the American continent that were subject to Spanish colonialism, the division between white Christians and black Christians has never been so sharp as in the United States.[4] The majority of black Christians in the United States belong to the "black church". These black churches are the oldest institutions formed by negroes in that country. Of the sixteen million black Christians fourteen million belong to church denominations created by the blacks themselves, and only two million to predominantly white denominations. In that context it is not surprising that a mere 800,000 blacks are members of the Catholic Church (1.7% of the total number of Catholics in the United States): the central structure of the Catholic Church really makes it impossible for blacks to achieve a Catholic Church of their

[4] Arnold J. Toynbee, "The Protestant Background of Our Modern Western Race Feeling", in *A Study of History* (London, 1934), pp. 211–27. Frank Tannenbaum, *Slave and Citizen—The Negro in the Americas* (New York, 1947), has shown that according to Anglo-American notions the slave was a *thing* and could make no claim to fundamental human rights such as marriage and capacity to form a contract. In the Spanish-Portuguese legal code the slave was a prisoner-of-war, who certainly did continue to be the subject of rights. His master was in duty bound to have him instructed in the Christian religion; his marriage was a sacrament and his family sacrosanct; he was legally capacious and could hold property; if he should pay back to his master the original price of his purchase, then he had to be set free. Erik von Kuehnelt-Leddihn, "Zur Rassenfrage in de Vereinigten Staaten", in *Hochland*, 62, 1 (Jan./Feb., 1970), pp. 56–67; Francis John Quinlivan, "New American Dream for Blacks", in *America* (9 May 1970), pp. 498–9.

own:[5] in the social rating of the white middle class in the United States "black Christianity" has been evaluated as a kind of second-class religion. On that score, one of Black Theology's primary tasks is to eliminate this division between white and black Christians. It would be pharisaical to behave as though white theology had nothing to learn from this process. One of the principal achievements of Black Theology is an expansion of Christian consciousness. But that entails a question for white theology too, regarding its own identity. It will be necessary on both sides to arrive at a renewed understanding of the Christian identity.

The "black" thinking that is a hallmark of Black Theology makes the white theologian aware of the extent to which his "universal" theological thinking is a myth: it has been a "white" mode of contemplating the Christian revelation. Thus Black Theology implies a process of renewal for black and white. It could lead to a new form of pluriformity in theology. It could lead to an integration of black theology with white; and it may lead to a revolutionary consciousness on the part of black Christians in the United States.

These are in fact the three main directions in which Black Theology is moving at the moment: and all three are very much of a piece with the three tendencies evident in black America at the present time: the movement towards integration, best and most clearly symbolized by the figure of Martin Luther King; a movement for a state within the state, for a church within the church, of a black nationalism, of a distinctively black culture and university education, which goes down particularly well with the young; a Marxist-oriented movement like that of the Black Panthers, of black militants and Black Power. The latter is certainly the most radical current of them all; and it poses as many

[5] The social standing of the various denominations in the United States is very sharply defined, even where whites themselves are concerned: the Episcopalians (Anglicans) rank as very high-class, like the Dutch Reformed (*Gereformeerden*); the Presbyterians enjoy just about the same status. Methodists and Christian Scientists come lower down the scale; and the Lutherans stand somewhere in between. Only in Maryland, Louisiana, New Mexico and California do Catholics have any sort of status; in the rest of the States a Catholic is seldom regarded as a real gentleman. This discrimination, too, is deliberately kept alive by what are known as the *Social Registers*, which include only people of the right sort.

problems for Black Theology as the revolutionary movements do for theology in general. For the consciousness of the bulk of these black militants the crucial turning-point came when on a dusty roadway in Mississippi, in the June of 1966, Stokely Carmichael raised the cry of Black Power. He reached the ear of an entire nation, touched the heart of the black man and uplifted it with new hope.[6] James Forman's Black Manifesto (of 4 May 1969) is evidently just a beginning. An influential group of activist black church leaders hailed the Manifesto as "just, humane and theologically correct": "Although white Christians will be shocked, this is a healing intervention by Christ himself." The second part of this statement may strike the theologian as a somewhat hasty utterance; but he will have to admit that the Manifesto has had a startling effect and has prompted many people to feel that once again the Church "as an ideological component of the Establishment" has come down on the wrong side of the (now black) revolution.

The question is how the black churches are going to understand their past and how Black Theology may help them to do that. The words of the Black Manifesto leave no doubt about it:[7] "The new black man wants to live and to live means that we must not become static or merely believe in self-defence. We must boldly go out and attack the white Western world at its power centres. The white Christian churches are another form of government in this country and they are used by the government of this country to exploit the people of Latin America, Asia and Africa; but the day is soon coming to an end.... But to win our demands from the church which is linked up with the United States Government, we must not forget that it will ultimately

[6] Walter R. Banks, "Two Impossible Revolutions? Black Power and Church Power", in *Journal for the Scientific Study of Religion*, VIII, 2 (Fall, 1969), pp. 263–8; Gary Maceoin, "The Church and the Black Man", in *National Catholic Reporter*, 15 (1970), appendix; Rosemary Ruether, "Education in Tandem: White Liberal, Black Militant", in *America* (May 1970), pp. 582–4; A.E., "Potere Negro", in Il Gallo (1969), nos. 7–8 (July–August), p. 139.
[7] A translation of the Black Manifesto appears in *IDOC International* (1969), no. 11, pp. 32–43; *Manifeste chrétien; IDOC Internazionale* (1970), no. 3, pp. 9–12: "Dichiarazione sul Black Power"; *De Bazuin* (31 Aug. 1969): "Het Zwarte Manifest" and *ibid.* (1970), no. 21, p. 8: "Kerkelijke reacties op het zwarte manifest".

be by force and power that we will win. We are not threatening the churches. We are saying that we know the churches came with the military might of the colonizers and have been *sustained* by the military might of the colonizers. Hence, if the churches in colonial territories were established by military might, we know deep within our hearts that we must be prepared to use force. . . . An attack on the religious beliefs of black people is not our major objective, even though we know that we were not Christians when we were brought to this country, but that Christianity was used to help enslave us. Our objective in issuing this Manifesto is to force the racist white Christian Church to begin the payment of reparations which are due to all black people, not only by the Church but also by private business and the U.S. Government. We see this focus on the Christian Church as an effort around which all black people can unite." They make an explicit claim to an overall control on behalf of all black people in the world. What they intend by "total control" is that black people who have suffered most from exploitation and racial discrimination must contrive to protect their interests as blacks by assuming the management of affairs in the United States. However, it is not enough that the black man should have his way. He must aim at building a new society: "Our hearts go out to the Vietnamese for we know what it is to suffer under the domination of racist America. Our heart, our soul and all the compassion we can mount goes out to our brothers in Africa, Santo Domingo, Latin America and Asia who are being tricked by the power structure of the United States. . . . We as black people must be concerned with the total conditions of all black people in the world."

Heart and soul and every degree of compassion will prove inadequate, unless conjoined with theological reflection. Where this Manifesto is concerned, it rests with Black Theology to point to two illusions: first, no more than anyone else can the black man reverse direction: it is illusory to look for a way back to African culture, and still more so to expect the black population of the world to see their problems embodied in the Black Revolution in the United States; second, the black man's discovery of his own identity cannot be an ultimate goal; it has to be an interim phase in a process of transcending both "black" and "white" thinking in a humane and Christian pluriformity, in a shared experiencing of Christian freedom. The black churches are not merely the oldest institution created by the negro in the United States— they are still the most influential; so that it is quite obviously a task of Black Theology to make the black churches thoroughly mobile: some—like Luther King's successor, the pragmatic and so far not very theologically oriented Jesse Jackson—desire this mobility for what they call "the black future"; others—the National Committee of Black Churchmen, for example—want no future in separation from whites, but rather a common future for white and black together. Jackson's pragmatic stance, "separate yet independent", is bound to aggravate the break in communication between white and black Christians, so as to remove all prospect of a Christian dialogue. One aim of Black Theology is precisely to make such a dialogue possible. This can only happen when Black Theology itself has a clear identity and when its partner in dialogue—let us call it, for convenience, White Theology—does not identify itself with that Black Theology. Professor John C. Bennett, of Union Seminary, is right when he says: "We cannot possibly allow ourselves to be paralysed by what our ancestors did to the negro. It must be sufficient to admit our solidarity with the collective sin of our contemporary society, which is controlled by whites. This society has failed to change its fundamental, racist patterns of behaviour and ways of implementing its policies in practice. It has not succeeded in delivering our black citizens from poverty and degradation, imposed on them by society even after the laws had been improved.... Unless events give us a jolt, we have no eyes to see, we remain indifferent, we procrastinate, we do little, where what needs to be done is a great deal."[8]

All this raises the big question to what extent the growing theological consciousness of the blacks in America may be said to afford an example to be followed by other black Christians—in Africa, for instance, where voices can also be heard clamouring for a *"théologie noire"*. In 1966 the NCBC (National Committee of Black Churchmen) set about establishing lines of contact with

[8] P. F. Th. Aalders, "Het geestelijk leiderschap van Union Seminary, New York", in *Wending* (September 1969), pp. 373-81; J. W. Schulte Nordholt, "Ethiek en praktijk van de geweldloosheid van Dr. Martin Luther King", in *Ethiek als Waagstuk* (Nijkerk, 1969), pp. 75-87.

the AACC (All Africa Conference of Churches). It is a new kind of "ecumene"; and it has come up against a whole lot of unforeseen snags. The black church of America is discovering that the black church of Africa has problems very different from its own to wrestle with. At first sight it might even appear that apart from the subordinate role to which they have been relegated by white Christians, they have no common problems at all. Significantly enough, when the NCBC asked the wealthy United Methodist Church (there are three main Methodist denominations in the United States, with one and a half million black members) for financial support, this was refused; but at the same time an unusually large sum was made over to the All Africa Conference of Churches. The African AACC still has highly respectful dealings with the rich white churches of America and, in contrast to the NCBC, wants to remain good friends with them. Yet it should be possible to bring the black churches of Africa, Latin America and the United States closer together. Or rather: their theological consciousness must not be manipulated by a "universal theology", so called, but must develop along its own lines into a joint reflection on a mode of being Christian that is distinctively its own.[9]

There are of course further and finer distinctions to be noted in what calls itself, in the context of the "Black Revolution", "Black Theology". However, sufficient elements have been presented already for us to repeat the question: Is this Black Theology a sign of hope?

## II. A SIGN OF HOPE?

An initial sign of hope is the fact that for the first time in history the black people of the United States are embarking on a style of Christian life in which they are at pains to reflect in their own way on their own religious mode of Christian experience. What has been said so far may seem to imply that the main target is white oppression. But there is more to it than that: there is the growth of a reflex consciousness that their style

[9] Gayroud S. Wilmore, Jr., "Africa and Afro-Americans", in *The Christian Century* (3 June 1970), p. 686; A. Sanon, "Communication sur les responsabilités de la théologie africaine", in *Revue du Clergé Africain*, XXIV, 3–4 (May–July 1969), pp. 337–50; L. Kaufmann, "Cincinnati, August 1969", in *Orientierung* (Sept. 1969), no. 17, pp. 181–4.

of Christian existence is different from that of the whites. Despite all the factors in white Christianity that stand in the way, this consciousness has become a fact which it is impossible to ignore; and it is an unlooked-for source of confirmation for the distinctive character, *qua* "church", of the black churches. It might well perturb us that out of thirty million American negroes only sixteen million are acknowledged members of the Christian churches; the churches have been undeniably the soundest gauges of the growth of black consciousness. It might also be thought perturbing that Black Theology should be so closely associated with Black Power; and one might get the impression that ultimately power is what it is all about. Thus it is not at all evident how grasping at power can be a sign of hope. Is power not rather a political factor, providing warranty for the future as "futurology"? Is the American dream of equality—attained by giving the same power to black and white—not rather a balance of forces, kept in being through fear of the power wielded by "the other side" than a way of bringing nearer the reign of God?

Cox[10] makes the point that theology nowadays has a concern with the convergence of social revolution and the growth of self-awareness and the tensions which this engenders. A convergence of that sort is obviously a distinctive mark of Black Theology; and so is a concern with the consequent tensions. Theology can no longer be envisaged as a fixed point of orientation in the landscape, from which one can reconnoitre and map out the surrounding country. We ought rather to be able to ask of it how effective it is in relation to the historical processes now operating. It is in this sense that Black Theology has its place in the process of emerging awareness on the part of the American negro and the consequent revolution, the issue of which it sees—probably mistakenly—as bringing nearer the messianic age. *How* that expectation is fulfilled is a secondary matter; the main thing is *that* it is being fulfilled. Of course, the further question arises at this point as to whether the fulfilment is a *true* one. But "true" does not indicate whether this fulfilling of a hope corresponds with a stipulated, *a priori* copy of something else. If it be asked: Is this

[10] Harvey Cox, "Politische Theologie", in *Evangelische Theologie*, no. 11 (Nov. 1969), p. 567.

true? then what is meant is: Can it survive the test of human experience in all its dimensions?

There is a third factor which prompts us to answer the question about Black Theology as a sign of hope in the affirmative: in white as well as black it engenders a real *conversio*, a real change of heart. On both sides a self-sufficiency is being overcome and a community is being changed, so that it has an opportunity, under however great a threat, to press on vigorously towards the next stage. There is no question of remaining content with a position where there are two kinds of churches, differing on grounds of colour and both claiming to be based on Christianity. It is quite possible that for the first time we can see ourselves confronted here with a divergence within Christianity which is kept going, not by any discrepancy of doctrine or belief but by two divergent life-styles, two tendencies each of which has need of the other, not just in order to make something fuller and richer of the *humanum* but to lend credibility to the Faith. We have had a white religious paternalism and a black religious servilism. The claim that God is a Father has been contaminated by that religious paternalism; and the conviction that the Son is also the Suffering Servant is infected with a religious servilism. Both convictions have to be disinfected, if the affirmations of God as the Father of all and of the Son as Redeemer, Deliverer and elder Brother are still to have an existential viability. It is not inconceivable that "to be disinfected" is a euphemism in this case, and that the biblical talk of dying to rise again would be more to the point.

It cannot be denied—and this is a fourth factor of hope in the bitter process of Black Theology—that the eye of faith is the cleaner and keener for having acquired the capacity to discover a new perspective.

Kierkegaard described hope as a passion for the possible.[11] That passion arises because God is known not only from the past, from history or from what is, here and now, but also from that which is yet to come, wherein we place our trust. It is *this* hope that lifts Christianity above the purely historical.

Black people have had everything knocked from their grasp.

[11] Sören Kierkegaard, *Philosophische Brocken* = Werke V (Rowohlt) (Munich, 1964), p. 79.

Yet for that very reason they are able to hope; and we cannot be surprised if so vital a hope as this at times converts the empty hand into the clenched fist of the revolutionary. Who knows whether in so doing they will not knock a great deal from the grasp of white Christianity and thus exonerate it from a self-sufficiency that restores to them the possibility of real hope.

*Translated by Hubert Hoskins*

Theo Lehmann

# A Cry of Hope—
# The Negro Spirituals

AT ALL times throughout human history, men who have lost their homeland have expressed their longing to return in song. The psalms of the exiled Israelites are, of course, an outstanding example of this, but the songs of the negro slaves living in North America had the same function as the psalms of Israel. They formed a bridge across into their lost homeland. This bridge not only led the North American negroes back into their old homeland in Africa, however—it also led them forward in a new direction. It took them over the "deep river" into a new homeland which was not on this earth. It led this oppressed people onwards in burning hope towards the "promised land where all is peace". These negro slaves longed and hoped to find a homeland on earth and in heaven, to achieve freedom from the slavery imposed by men and by sin and to attain peace and justice here and now and in eternity. This hope was united and expressed in the spiritual songs which became the negroes' great cry for redemption. Earthly and heavenly aspirations were inseparably mixed in their faith and this faith was reflected in the negro spirituals—the bridge which led the negroes through their period of slavery.

## I. THE NEGRO CHURCH

On the one hand, the period of slavery was undoubtedly one of the darkest in the history of the Church. On the other hand, however, the emergence of the negro Church in the eighteenth century and its enormous growth in the nineteenth was also one of the most significant events in Christian history. The nineteenth century was, of course, the great missionary century. When this great period of missionary activity came to a close in 1914, the Protestant Churches had almost as many members among the American negroes as they had among all the people in Africa and Asia put together.[1] In other words, all the work done by European and American missionaries in the whole accessible world produced no higher quantitative results than the activity carried out among the negroes of America. By 1914, the number of American negro Christians had reached two-thirds of the total of all Roman Catholic converts in Africa and Asia. What is more, it should not be forgotten that missionary work had been going on among the Asian and African peoples for centuries. This contrasts sharply with the missionary situation among the American negroes—the vital missionary consciousness of the negroes themselves meant that the conversion of the American negroes went ahead with the speed and impetus of an avalanche.

The most remarkable aspect of the emergence of the negro Church was that it took place while the negroes were still slaves and that oppressed people, in other words, were accepting the faith of their oppressors. The white oppressors strove to tell their slaves as far as possible only those parts of the Bible which would strengthen their own authority and which would help to keep the negroes humble, submissive and obedient. It cannot be denied that the white masters had considerable success in this, but it would at the same time be wrong to hold Christianity responsible for what the white representatives of Christianity passed on to their black slaves as the biblical message. These slaves were, of course, illiterate and could not read the Bible themselves. What they were given was a selection from the Bible. The negroes were taught humbly to acknowledge their submission to their white masters and any revolutionary ideas that they might have had were stifled—all with the help of the Bible. But it was, of course, a shortened Bible used as an instrument to reinforce the authority of the ruling class or race. The so-called slave revolts are proof of the great revolutionary force that was derived from the Bible as

---

[1] K. S. Latourette, *The Great Century in Europe and the United States of America, 1800–1914* (New York, 1941), p. 341.

soon as the negroes themselves were able to read it as a whole.[2] What is more, the negroes tried to justify these slave revolts by quotations and evidence from the Bible in precisely the same way as their white masters supported their theory that the negroes were inferior. There is no question here of a black exegesis being in opposition, as it were, to a white exegesis; what we have is rather two aspects of the Bible being played off against each other. In any case, what is shown with great clarity by these revolts is that the Bible could no longer be used—or misused—as an instrument of suppression as soon as the negroes had learnt to read it themselves. In the hands of the negroes themselves, the Bible became a dangerous weapon and indeed the main basis of their demands for freedom. The most decisive consequence of these revolts was therefore that laws were passed in several states forbidding negroes to learn how to read. Especially after Nat Turner's rebellion,[3] they were also forbidden to preach, their meetings were strictly controlled by the whites, and so on. By reacting to the revolts by forbidding the negroes to learn how to read and to use the Bible independently, the white Americans made one clear practical admission. They acknowledged that it was not an essential part of the biblical message to make men into pliant and submissive subjects, but that this message, of its very nature, acted as a counter pressure against all oppression and resulted in a call to freedom. We are bound therefore to conclude that it was not their Christian faith as such which paralysed the negroes' power to resist and which made them submit patiently to their fate. On the contrary, the Christian faith they had been given was clearly one which had been distorted and pruned by the slave-owners for their own purposes.

## II. The Part played by the Bible in the Fight for Freedom

The Bible was dynamite in the hands of the slaves, endangering the position of the privileged white men and giving rise to a potential revolutionary situation. The Christian faith was the most powerful force in the negroes' fight for freedom. This fact has been overlooked by everyone who identifies the Christian

[2] H. Aptheker, *American Negro Slave Revolts* (New York, 1964[5]).
[3] H. Aptheker, *Nat Turner's Slave Rebellion* (New York, 1966).

negro with the legendary figure of Uncle Tom and who rejects everything that has to do with slavery—including Christianity. There have been times when the negroes themselves have repudiated their spirituals because they originated during the tragic period of slavery. This is a perfectly understandable reaction. In the meantime, however, a different view of history has been developing and a different light is also being thrown on the part played by Christianity in the negro's struggle to establish his identity, in his way of thinking about his past and in his political and social achievements. It is a fact that the Bible was a more important means than any other in the hands of the slave owners of oppressing and, as in the classic case of Uncle Tom, of domesticating the negro slave. On the other hand, however, it is equally a fact that the same negroes have the same Bible to thank for all the essentially revolutionary impulses in their fight for freedom— from its earliest beginnings right up to the present struggle for civil rights. The history of the American negro would have followed quite a different course if the Bible had played no part in it. With the Bible, however, the negro has had a source of constant strength which has decisively influenced the destiny of his people and has formed the lasting basis of his fight for freedom.

The negroes learned to understand the meaning of human dignity from the image of man given to them by the Bible. In contrast to the official teaching of their white masters, the Bible taught them that every man had the dignity of a being created by God and that all men were equal before God. This knowledge was, of course, of immeasurable importance to people whose white masters refused to allow them to live a life that was worthy of man because of the colour of their skin and never ceased to tell them that they were inferior and cursed by God. This white teaching was "proved" by philosophers and theologians in their books[4] and the slave owners translated these learned treatises into practical terms with the help of the whip. It was from this winepress of slavery that the negro spirituals flowed like a cry from the depths, at the same time expressing the hope, the great faith and the longing for freedom of the whole people.

The basic experience of the American negro and the

[4] H. Hughes, *Treatise on Sociology, Theoretical and Practical* (Philadelphia, 1954); J. Priest, *A Bible Defense of Slavery* (Louisville, 1864).

fundamental melody of all that he wanted to express in song, from the spirituals, via the blues[5] to jazz and modern negro lyrics, was suffering. The counterpoint to this cry from the depths has been a cry of hope and the triumphant certainty of redemption. This hope of redemption is especially clearly expressed, for example, in the well-known spiritual "Nobody knows the trouble I've seen," a song in which God is praised resoundingly from the great depths of human suffering.

### III. Cry from the Depths

In the context in which he discussed his conversion to Christianity, Heinrich Heine also considered the famous book *Uncle Tom's Cabin* and described in a most striking way the negro's understanding of the Bible: "A poor negro slave like this also reads with his back and therefore understands much better than we do."[6] The crucified, suffering Christ in fact occupied a central position in the spirituals of these negro slaves, whose hope was nourished especially by the Old Testament accounts of God's saving acts. They were above all interested in those biblical stories which told of God intervening in human history and setting men free from their distress. The same themes that played such an important part in the art of the catacombs in the very earliest days of the Church are also dominant in the negro spirituals. Noah in the ark, Jonah in the belly of the whale, Daniel in the lion's den and the three young men in the fiery furnace—these figure especially in the spirituals. Above all, however, the negroes sang about the deliverance of the people of Israel from the power of Pharaoh. They at once recognized their own fate in the biblical accounts of the history of Israel, the exile and slavery of the people of God in Egypt and their ultimate liberation from their oppressors. It was also inevitable that they should say to themselves, if this God, who once saved his people from slavery, is living, why should he not save his negro people from slavery as well? And so they hoped that God would send them a Moses too and sang that most majestic of all spirituals, "Go down, Moses".
The fate of the negro people was in so many ways so similar

[5] T. Lehmann, *Blues and Trouble* (Berlin, 1966).
[6] H. Heine, *Geständnisse* (Hamburg, 1868), p. 293.
9—C.

to that of the people of Israel that a comparison between their songs is something that can be taken for granted. The spirituals are in fact very close to the psalms in many respects, but in one important respect they are very different. Whereas Psalm 137, for example, ends on a note of hatred and vengeance, the songs of the negro slaves, whose suffering can only be compared with that of the people of Israel, rise up in pure praise of God and contain no trace of hatred of the oppressor and no indication of any desire for vengeance. These songs were born of the very spirit of Christ, who suffered without hating his oppressors. They are songs in the spirit of the New Testament—songs of the Holy Spirit.

## IV. The Integral Nature of the Spiritual

Arnold Toynbee regarded the negro spirituals as a significant spiritual response to the challenge evoked by material degradation and slavery. The spiritual character of these songs is most clearly heard, of course, in their eschatological themes. The second coming of Christ, the last judgment, the resurrection from the dead and heaven—it is in these themes that the negro slaves' passionate hope and expectation of a better future are most distinctly expressed. Freedom from sin and freedom from slavery become one in them and it would be quite wrong to separate this desire for freedom, which is voiced in such a complex way in the negro spirituals, and place it on two different levels. There is no question of two separate concepts of freedom, one "secular" and the other "spiritual", in these songs. There is only one idea of freedom and this contains both secular and spiritual aspects. It would therefore be a mistake to interpret the negro spirituals in a one-sided manner, on the one hand as purely secular protest songs which simply make use of religious terminology or, on the other, as purely religious songs which simply express a longing to be free from the bondage of sin. Anyone who believes that there is a sharp division or antithesis between the "secular" and the "spiritual" in these songs has clearly misunderstood their integral nature. The secular and the spiritual elements are inextricably interwoven in them and it is precisely their integral character which constitutes their distinctive quality. This integral character is most apparent in the musical form of the spiritual and in its relationship with jazz, which presents itself as a unity of secular and religious or spiritual music.[7] This is also the point at which the negro spirituals become our most powerful hope for the Church's new and contemporary music.

## V. A Gift to World Christianity

The spirituals are not only the negroes' most important contribution to the culture of America—they are also a valuable contribution to the musical life of the Church and therefore a precious gift to world Christianity. Heinz Werner Zimmermann has called them "the most significant achievement in the field of Church music in the nineteenth century".[8] In a later publication, he drew attention to the fact that, "Just as the stream of musical creation was drying up in Europe, another began to flow almost independently and a long way away".[9] The negro spirituals originated in the eighteenth and nineteenth centuries in the crucible of the religious revival which was at that time sweeping across America and drawing the negroes as well into its vortex. The consequence of this was that the spirituals were a mixture of African and European traditions based on a common practice of singing, especially that of evocation and response by the people. As a result, they cannot be traced back either to Africa or to Europe exclusively. They are a product, inseparably mixed, of both societies.[10] To begin with, this process of mixing went ahead quite unobserved and, when the spirituals were sung for the first time in Europe, they were not heard in their original form, but performed in a concert arrangement by the choir of Fisk University, the Fisk Jubilee Singers.[11] It was not until after the Second World War that Europe came to know the original form of the

[7] T. Lehmann, *Negro Spirituals, Geschichte und Theologie* (Berlin, 1965).

[8] H. W. Zimmermann, *Kirchenmusik heute*, Behrend/Uhde, Prisma der gegenwärtigen Musik (Hamburg, 1959), p. 242.

[9] H. W. Zimmermann, "Neue Musik und Kirchenlied", in *Musik und Gottesdienst*, 6 (1962), p. 156.

[10] H. Lilje, K. H. Hansen, S. Schmidt-Joos, *Das Buch der Spirituals und Gospel Songs* (Hamburg, 1961).

[11] J. B. T. Marsh, *The Story of the Jubilee Singers, with their Songs* (London, 1877).

negro spirituals to any great extent and this took place first of all
through the medium of jazz. Long before Europeans became
aware in their churches of the existence of the negro spirituals—
in their modern, jazz-like form, they are known as gospel songs
—melodies such as "When the saints go marching in" and "Down
by the riverside" formed part of the standard repertory of countless Dixieland bands. Furthermore, the wave of gospel songs
in the nineteen-sixties helped negro spirituals to become international property, even if only in the watered down form of
popular songs.

## VI. Hope for the Church Song of the Future

Many attempts have been and are still being made in Europe
to find new kinds of song to be sung in church and it was, of
course, inevitable that increasing interest should be shown in the
negro spiritual. Christians, and especially young Christians, have
become more and more dissatisfied with traditional church
songs, both from the point of view of their texts and from that
of their melodies. The demand for a completely new kind of
liturgical song has consequently become louder and more insistent. This has resulted in a constant search for new songs with
texts and musical scoring which really express the twentieth-cen-
tury Christian's experience of faith and understanding of the
world. The negro spirituals have played and are still playing a
central part in this creative process. They have not entirely ceased
to be created. On the contrary, they are still being produced today according to the same basic principles that were observed a
hundred years ago, but they have taken on a form which has become an essential part of the musical idiom of the contemporary
world. The wave of folk songs which began in America has now
become international. Each country has, as it were, given its own
national flavour to the folk song without, however, making any
fundamental changes in its basic structure. The "American way
of singing" is no longer regarded in Europe as a foreign import—
it is fully accepted as a style which determines the musical
climate. In view of this, it is only natural that composers of contemporary songs for the Church should also make use of this
musical idiom, especially as the point of departure and the very

essence of this kind of singing are in fact the church song itself, in this case, the spirituals of the North American negro.

In the first wave of enthusiasm, these negro spirituals were either taken over just as they were or else closely imitated. This is, however, neither desirable nor practicable. As far as the texts of the spirituals are concerned, these usually present a very great obstacle to most Europeans if only because of the ideas and symbols they contain. The attempts that have so far been made to provide translations that can be sung easily have therefore proved unsatisfactory. As far as the music is concerned, experience has taught us that negro spirituals can only be genuinely interpreted and sung by relatively few educated and gifted Europeans. This is simply not possible in the case of whole church communities.

If, then, pure imitation is out of the question, there is still the possibility of taking over the melodies and singing them to completely new texts. There are several very successful examples of this practice, although it would not be possible to speak of negro spirituals in the narrow sense of the word or of absolutely authentic interpretations. This, however, is not the most important aspect of the question. What is important is that the end-product is a song which satisfies the demands of contemporary man as far as the melody is concerned, which can be sung easily by everyone and which carries everyone irresistibly along. There are more than enough songs of this kind among the negro spirituals and they are simply waiting to be provided with a new text so that they can take their place in the ecumenical repertory of church songs. The negro spirituals are not simply a cry of hope coming down to us now from the remote past. They are also a hope for the church song of the future.

*Translated by David Smith*

David Bradley

# The Western Crisis and the Attraction of Asian Religions

TO STATE that the West is living through a crucial period is a truism for readers of this journal. This current crisis is the culmination of a lingering malaise. The sickness of our society has many contributing factors and displays a syndrome of ailments which involves every aspect of human existence, both personal and social. Much has been written on possible causes and cures for this illness, but the interacting forces which contribute to it remain difficult to fathom since they are as complex and elusive as human nature itself. At the same time this "crisis of the spirit" might be brought into clearer focus if it is examined in the light of a particular facet of the contemporary scene. One such facet is found in the current fascination on the part of large numbers of Europeans and North Americans for the cultures and religions of Asia. This interest is closely related to a growing discontent on the part of many with the values and norms of Western culture. In this article I would like to analyse four possible causes for this discontent along with a brief discussion of some of the forms this interest in things Asian is taking, concluding with an evaluation of its validity and relative importance.

## FOUR CAUSES OF WESTERN DISCONTENT

One cause of discontent is to be found among those millions of persons whose lives have been uprooted by the forces of war and social change. Two major wars and many smaller ones have caused the disruption of countless families by death from battle, famine and disease, as well as through the physical destruction of homes and communities. Large numbers of refugees have settled in new areas, often far from their homelands. There also has been an increasing mobility of persons due to such things as the migration of farmers to urban centres and to changing patterns of employment in an increasingly industrialized society. One can picture, e.g., a young soldier from a middle European country returning to his ancestral home in 1945 after years of cruel war. Perhaps he is a Roman Catholic now married to a Protestant girl from an enemy nation. He finds that his parents were killed during the war, his family's business is ruined and he himself is not welcomed by his relatives due to his interfaith marriage. Now twenty-five years later the children of this couple share some of the sense of rootlessness of their parents.

Or consider the typical displaced person who has moved from a farm to a huge city where he finds no true neighbourhood and most of his everyday contacts are with faceless strangers. As modern technology broadens its influence over society the city dweller loses his sense of identity and becomes a cipher. He is assigned a number and he votes, is hired and fired, and even buried by reference to this number. Such persons often are unable to cope with problems which would have posed no difficulty in the context of the communal relationships of his traditional family and village life. This lack of usual relationships and loyalties makes him easy prey to the blandishments of totalitarian philosophers which call men to a "higher" loyalty to a special class, race or national state. But many of those who long for a sense of community, fellowship and peace in a chaotic world turn instead to the religions of Asia.

This sense of rootlessness and depersonalization is accentuated by the decline of traditional goals and values which makes one vulnerable to the fears and sense of hopelessness so prevalent in our technological society. The Judeo-Christian tradition has experienced a continual erosion of the biblical eschatology with its promise of a future secure in God's hands. Recent scientific developments have intensified the centuries-old challenge to traditional faith, while such events as the moon landings have shaken, even for the most orthodox, literal belief in a spatial heaven and hell and have helped to increase scepticism about a future life without making available any substitute for the older hope. The widespread sense of dread of atomic war, and, in America, the fact of the military draft and continuing madness of war in South-East Asia, have caused many to live only for the moment and to abandon religious sanctions for the traditional morality. Inside the Church this relativity has found expression in the "new morality" and the "death of God" schools. Another indication of the pervasiveness of this sense of impending doom and hopelessness is found in the phenomenal growth of interest in astrology, horoscopes and divination of the future in various forms. By such means many seek to acquire meaning and power for their lives which they have not found in the biblical tradition. Others turn to drugs to simulate religious experience, while yet others turn to Asian religions in search of meaning and goals for their impoverished lives.

Every great culture exhibits a strong measure of pride in its achievements. Yet in the West, along with such pride, there seems to be an inordinate amount of self-criticism, and even of revulsion against our culture. The anomaly of so-called Christian nations engaging in countless wars over the centuries, culminating in two world wars sponsored essentially by these same nations, needs no comment. The widespread racism, either sanctioned or even championed by sections of Christianity, along with the linking of colonialism in Asia, Africa and South America with the Christian nations of Europe has led to Christianity being regarded as a white man's religion on the part of most members of the coloured races. But scientism and humanism, two movements often found in opposition to the Church, also have come under criticism. The notion of gradual but inevitable progress under the twin banners of humanism and science has lost much of its appeal. Science has made possible many marvellous things but also has produced atomic and bio-chemical warfare, and has helped to produce a technological society wherein man is reduced to the level of machines. The humanist tradition has helped produce a high degree of literacy, mass education, helped eliminate slavery and colonialism, and, along with science, eradicated much disease and made possible wealth and leisure for more millions than ever before. Yet among those same persons who have benefited most from economic and technological advances there is widespread unhappiness, much alcoholism, divorce, suicide and murder, there is carnage on the highways and millions live in poverty. The science and humanism which promised to create a utopia are mocked by monstrous problems of pollution, population pressure and continued war. Once again, the person who rejects amoral science and hollow humanism often turns from Western culture in disgust and looks to Asia for possible answers.

A fourth expression of discontent is found in the rejection of authority on the part of our young people. In the 1930s the Hitler *Jugend* fled the authority of parent, school teacher and pastor. They would leave home and travel in groups seeking a new communal life wherein they would attempt to create their own ideals and exercise their own authority. They also sought to translate this movement into a new political force. In the 1970s there is widespread rebellion on the part of large numbers of our youth against their parents. The nature, value and purpose of education is called in question and the Church, with its claims to authority, is either attacked or ignored by these same young people. Along with this rejection of home, school and church is found a growing criticism of Western political institutions, and the call to idealistic youth has gone out to revolt against constitutional democracy. Here again one finds a turning to Asia on the part of many who assume that there one can find freedom from parental domination, escape the trap of education geared for life in a technological society, and the authority of a dogma-ridden Church.

## THE ATTRACTION OF ASIAN RELIGIONS

During the past hundred years several generations of scholars have laboured to translate the major religious texts of India, China and Japan into European languages so that they are easily available. Authors such as Somerset Maugham, Hermann Hesse, Alan Watts and Aldous Huxley have popularized their insights into the message and challenge of Asian religions. The Hindu and Buddhist missionaries and spiritual teachers who have for decades infiltrated the West have, in recent years, achieved spectacular success in attracting followers, especially from among influential members of the entertainment world. With knowledge about the religions of Asia easily available, and with groups of enthusiastic believers propagating these faiths, many who have known only the biblical tradition are now presented with real options to their traditional faith. They are now turning to Asia for help in facing the problems created by life in our modern technological age. What they find attractive can be summarized under four categories roughly matching the four causes of discontent discussed above.

It is human nature to assume that "the grass is greener on the other side", and many who find themselves stifled by life in an urbanized, technological society are turning to Asia in search of their lost identities. Sometimes this takes the physical form of an actual pilgrimage to the lands of the Himalayas or the River Ganges. And for the stay-at-home this desire for himself what Asia has to offer might take the form of reading the Buddhist *Dhammapada*, or the Hindu *Bhagavad-Gita* or *The Upanishads*. There they discover moral beauty and spiritual teachings that they did not know existed. Whereas frequently the Bible remains a closed book to them they find in these scriptures much that is most appealing. Another example of the attraction of Asian religion is found in the career of Mahatma Gandhi. Not only did he follow Indian teachings of non-violence and soulforce to lead his people to independence, but he also inspired the Christian leader Martin Luther King to lead the American negro towards equality. Though it is true that Dr. King was a Baptist minister, the Ku Klux Klan also claims to represent true Christianity and the influence of Gandhi remains dominant in the minds of many. The rise of the Black Muslim movement in America owes most of its success to a message of Muslim brotherhood that makes it possible for an American black to hold his head high and to have a sense of freedom and self-importance that he did not find as a Christian. In such ways the "spiritual" East holds a positive message for many who feel themselves trapped in the "materialistic" West.

The current "death of God" school and the "new morality" are both symptomatic of the degree to which traditional sanctions, goals and hopes have evaporated leaving a spiritual vacuum. But instead of following the latest theological fads many have turned to the East for substitutes for the older eschatology. Many have studied Zen Buddhism and for some it has proven itself as a way of life that truly answers their needs. Others have turned to various aspects of Yoga, and even to a study of the *Tibetan Book of the Dead*, partly because of interest sparked by writings on this text by the psychiatrist C. G. Jung. The increase in Europe and America in the use of hashish and psychedelic drugs undoubtedly reflects the widespread sense of frustration and need for an escape from the smothering nature of our society, but there also is a clear connection with Asian religions. Drugs are linked with various Asian cults and the Eastern stress on mystical experience has led many to assume that one can find a short-cut to mystical experience by this route.

One widespread substitute for biblical faith is found in the use of horoscopes and the practising of various forms of necromancy and astrology. This actually is part of the tissue of the cultures of South and East Asia. One form of divination that has become almost a cult in the West is the use of the Chinese classic, the *I Ching* or *Book of Changes*. Richard Wilhelm's German translation and its English rendering by Cary Baynes (including a long *Introduction* by C. G. Jung) has had heavy sales, among American College students, and many thousands now use the *I Ching* as a guide for daily living.

A third category includes those revolted by Western militarism, racism and materialism. For such the Indian teaching of *ahimsa*, not-harming or non-violence, used so effectively by Gandhi, is most attractive. The negative examples of the American Ku Klux Klan or of Apartheid in South Africa mean for them that Christianity has become essentially a white man's religion. On the other hand, Buddhism is found appealing because it is not tainted with a record of colonialism and constant warfare. For those who feel guilty about the possession of wealth while over half the world's peoples never have enough to eat, Asia represents a place where one can escape the materialism and greed felt to characterize the West.

Finally, for those who have revolted against authority, Asian religions represent the opportunity of self-salvation free of the oppressive dogmas of the authoritarian revelations of the biblical religions. Buddhism offers religion free from such dogmas while Hinduism presents itself as tolerant in contrast to the biblical stress on choice between belief and damnation. The biblical doctrine of a creator God and of man as lord of nature is blamed for the destruction of natural beauty and to the present crisis of pollution. On the other hand the Chinese philosophy of Taoism teaches harmony with nature as the ideal way. The Asian emphasis on freedom of the spirit and of religion as a path to harmony and peace is most attractive.

## SOME IRONIES INVOLVED IN THIS TURNING TO ASIA

The attraction of Asian religions is one that bristles with ironies. In discussions with my students I find that they idealize Asian culture, perhaps to the degree that they are revolted by their own culture. Such persons seldom are aware that Asia too is caught up in a crisis equal to that of the West. One who is concerned about the submersion of the individual in our modern society will find the same problem everywhere in Asia. So too, in spite of its ideal of non-violence, India remains a most violent country with a grim record of personal and social discord and cruel conflict. The vicious Hindu-Muslim riots in Ahmedabad in the autumn of 1969 or the continual violence in Calcutta are but recent examples of the sort of indescribable violence which erupted between Pakistan and India at the time of partition in 1947.

One who turns to Asia for relief from the vexing racial conflicts in the West immediately comes up against the same sort of man's inhumanity to man. The caste distinctions in India, although outlawed in the National Constitution, nevertheless continue as part of the daily life of most Indians. Racial and religious discrimination are widespread in Pakistan, Ceylon and Japan even though it often is covered over and not too apparent to the casual visitor. There is real irony in the fact that while educated Asians participate in the "brain-drain" to the West idealistic young Westerners from many countries make significant personal sacrifices in volunteer service to Asians whom they consider to be underprivileged. It is accurate to state that the usual attitude of Asians towards Westerners is one of envy. People are much the same everywhere and one should not be surprised to learn that there is much more materialistic greed than "spirituality" in Asia just as there is in the West.

The Westerner who chafes under discipline and authority often turns to Zen thinking to find freedom and release from responsibility. But if he is serious he soon learns how rigorous are the demands of Zen for self-discipline to achieve total control of one's life. And to mention one final irony, many who reject biblical mythology and prayer often appear eager to believe in divination, Asian astrology and the mythologies of Hinduism and Mahayana Buddhism.

## THE ROLE OF THE CHURCH

Although the term crisis would appear to fit our situation it might be of some comfort to remember that in the early days of Christianity there was a similar "loss of nerve" in the Greco-Roman world to which the Church addressed itself with success. Christianity was able to compete with religions which involved ways of self-salvation, the practice of divination and astrology, and with the goal of life as one of seeking harmony with the world of nature. Over the centuries the Church has continued to respond to similar challenges and to offer a message which offers meaning to persons who feel smothered by the realities of life. This is partly because Christianity has continued to carry within itself the powers necessary for self-renewal. There is a constant danger that the Gospel might be captured and imprisoned by the institution of the Church so that Church doctrine is substituted for the power of the truth of God. But when a danger such as the one here described—the attraction of Asian religions to Christians—represents a failure on the part of the Church to minister to the needs of its followers there always have been those ready to work for necessary change and reform.

This statement about self-renewal of the Church as it has worked in the past, however, might be too optimistic in the face of this particular crisis. It is a fact that in spite of openness to change throughout the Church very little is being done by the Church to inform its members about the nature and value of Asian religions. Is it not possible that this admittedly difficult and dangerous subject is like that of the understanding of sex? If the young person does not learn about sex in the home or in the Church he certainly will learn about it elsewhere. So if one learns about the appeal of Eastern faiths only from his peers he is quite likely to follow the example of growing numbers of his kind, follow the lure of the Orient, and turn his back on Christianity.

# PART III
## DOCUMENTATION
## CONCILIUM

Concilium General Secretariat

# The Dialectic of Hope and Despair

ANY number of a periodical which is devoted to a central theme has the disadvantage that it may lead to a narrowing of perspective. This holds also for an issue, which, like the present one, concentrates on hope.[1]

It creates the impression that we can see the whole of reality in the perspective of hope. But the plain observation of anyone truly involved in our present society already contradicts this view. Together with the undeniable signs of growing hopefulness there is a not less impressive list of facts and convictions that seem to justify a perspective of despair.

[1] This applies to the sciences, too. Each science must methodologically limit itself to its method and object, but this narrows the perspective. Even if theology considered it its task to correct this narrowing of perspective in the sciences, it should always remain aware that it is equally exposed to this evil itself as a science. Cf. E. Leppin, "Denkmodelle des Glaubens", in *Zeitschr. f. Theol. u. Kirche*, 66, 2 (July 1969), pp. 210–44, esp. p. 240: "III Bedeutung und Gebrauch der Denkmodelle". If faith is not going to withdraw into an ecclesiastical ghetto and to rest content with a consensus among similar-minded people, we should remember W. W. Bartley's observation (*Flucht ins Engagement*, 1962, pp. 161–2) that the theologian should not try to provide a pan-rational vindication of the faith on the one hand, and, on the other, should not exempt any of his starting-points from criticism under the pretext that belief or a non-rational commitment can be taken, without further justification, as a principle on which to base a view which, for the rest, cannot stand up to criticism. Cf. H. Grass, *Theologie und Kritik* (Göttingen, 1969); K. P. Popper, *The Logic of Scientific Discovery* (London, 1959); E. Schillebeeckx, "Het 'rechte' geloof, zijn onzekerheden en criteria", in *Tijdschr. v. Theol.*, 9 (1969), pp. 125–50 (with summary); S. Ijsseling, "De verwevenheid van universiteit en theologie", in *Tijdschr. v. Theol.*, 10, 2 (1970), pp. 123–38 (with summary).

The aim of this documentation is to put some of these facts and convictions, in so far as we find them in contemporary theological literature, into a convenient and pastorally useful survey. Thus we hope to bring some balance into the otherwise necessarily one-sided treatment of hope and to create an opportunity for a dialectic between hope and despair to come to life.

## I. Despair

Most modern dictionaries or lexica[2] refer the reader from the key-word "despair" to "hope". This gives the impression as if despair were merely an appendage to the notion of hope, or the waste-material coming from the hope-factory, or at most simply the logical counterpart of hope.

Since Sartre's philosophy of life as a futile concern (*passion inutile*)[3] and Camus's persuasive exposé of man's existence as basically nonsense (*non-sens*),[4] however, some try to legitimate despair as a pattern of life in its own right, which can be justified just as well as hope.

It is curious that after such philosophical reflections on despair as a pattern of life in its own right in the style of Sartre and Camus, hope again emerges as the principle of a philosophy about reality in an author like Bloch. It is still more striking that both

[2] Thus, among others, *Lex. f. Theol. u. Kirche*, s.v. "Verzweiflung" and *Dict. de Spiritualité*, s.v. "Désespoir". Cf. H. Widmer, "Zum Begriff der Erwartung und Hoffnung bei Laín Entralgo", in *Freiburger Zeitschr. f. Phil. u. Theol.*, 16, 3 (1969), pp. 428–54; *Theologisch Woordenboek*, s.v. "Wanhoop".

[3] "Thus man's passion is the inverse of Christ's, for man loses himself so that God may be born. But the idea of God is contradictory and we lose ourselves in vain; man is a futile passion" (in the French edn., *L'Etre et le Néant*, Paris, 1943, p. 708).

[4] "The absurd is the essential idea and the first truth", in *Le mythe de Sisyphe*, p. 49; "I want to have everything explained or nothing. And reason is incapable of answering this cry from the heart.... The absurd is born of this confrontation between this appeal of man and the senseless silence of the world", *loc. cit.*, pp. 44 and 45. Heidegger himself rejects the explanation of what he has said about *"Angst"* as leading in the direction of existentialism and implying a similar absurdity, yet his *Sein zum Tode* and his *Geworfenheit* seem to come to the same conclusion: "Anxiety is ... the feeling that our original situation reveals that we have been thrown into the world to die there", in A. de Waehlens, *La philosophie de M. Heidegger*, p. 121.

sides see in hope and despair respectively an ultimate principle. Neither side seems to go beyond this and to try to find a rational basis for either.[5]

It would be too superficial to attribute this element of finality simply to some basic pessimism or optimism.[6] One cannot really by-pass the problem why people see in hope or despair a *principle*. And by *principle* we mean here a starting-point which cannot be explained any further within the system adopted.

So one wonders whether the fact that these starting-points cannot be further explained has something to do with a broader context were all the cultural and sociological data to play their part.

Those who take hope as their fundamental principle are not blind to the reasons why people of only one generation back opted explicitly for despair as their fundamental principle. Perhaps they explain this too glibly with the argument of cultural philosophy that when a given phase of culture comes to an end it becomes biologically conditioned by despair. In that case despair would simply be an emotion that is sociologically determined. Bloch's followers would then simply say that existentialism is the last philosophy of a bourgeois culture. Now that this bourgeois society is being overtaken by a socialist, or Marxist, society, there is room for a new philosophy and a new starting-point: hope.[7]

[5] W. D. Marsch, *Hoffen worauf?* (Hamburg, 1963). In this matter Sartre, Camus, Heidegger and Bultmann all owe a debt to S. Kierkegaard's *Die Krankheit zum Tod*, where despair as an autonomous pattern of life is analysed and ultimately rejected, though he points to a kind of despair that leads to faith: "The false doubt doubts everything, and not only the person himself, while the saving doubt only makes the person doubt himself with the help of faith", in *Erbauliche Reden* (1843/4), p. 35. P. H. Chombart de Lauwe, *Pour une sociologie des Aspirations*. Eléments pour des perspectives nouvelles en Sciences Humaines (Paris, 1969); P. M. de Jong, "De bronnen van de ene menswetenschap", I, II and III, in *Streven* (Dec. 1969), pp. 286–94 and (Jan. 1970), pp. 402–11; a good example of dialectic cohesion of hope and despair, success and failure, may be found in D. Vasse, *Le temps du désir* (Paris, 1969).

[6] R. Bultmann, "Optimismus und Pessimismus in Antike und Christentum", in *Universitas* (Stuttgart, 1961), pp. 811–33; J. Pieper, *Ueber die Hoffnung* (Munich, 6th edn., 1949), pp. 13 and 38; Lain Entralgo, *La espera y la esperanza* (3rd edn., Madrid, 1962) and *Teoria y realidad del otro* (Madrid, 1961).

[7] See, among others, E. Bloch, *Das Prinzip Hoffnung* (3—T. Ausgabe, Frankfurt a. M., 1968), pp. 503, 787, 1617.

In the beginning of this documentation we referred to a narrowing of perspective, and this seems to operate also in this argument. One might say, with Bloch, that matter itself is the ultimate foundation of hope for the future because of its co-operation with man and its willing readiness to be handled by anyone approaching it with a human intent. But such a consideration would not cover the whole of reality unless one starts by taking for granted that the future in all its universality will be the product of Marxist historical materialism in its new dress.

The article on Black Theology in this number shows already that this kind of optimism can hardly be justified. Hope, as a principle, is more of a problem than authors of this school care to admit.[8]

Nor is it a satisfactory argument to say that we have to start somewhere if we want to approach reality as a whole, for the question remains why this particular point is chosen as the starting-point. That hope constitutes the only starting-point is not exactly self-evident for everybody, no more than despair. If either is nevertheless taken as the starting-point, as *principle*, one appeals too quickly to the old self-evident first principles of scholasticism.

On the other hand, everyone can see that hope and despair imply such more fundamental ethical principles as trust and distrust,[9] and this trust and distrust with regard to reality can be argued, at least in a modern ethic of growing consciousness.

## II. Sociology of Theology

Although, side by side with a philosophy of history and a philosophy of sociology, some authors have begun to work in the direction of a theology of history[10] and a theology of sociology,[11] there is still hardly any mention of a sociology of theology.

[8] W. Pannenberg, "Der Gott der Hoffnung", in *Ernst Bloch zu Ehren* Frankfurt, 1965), pp. 209–25 and T. Altizer, *The Gospel of Christian Atheism* (Philadelphia, 1966), pp. 18, 82, 105 f.

[9] G. Hasenhüttl, *Der Glaubensvollzug* (Essen, 1963), p. 255: "Der Glaube als Hoffnung".

[10] J. M. Robinson and J. B. Cobb (ed.), *Theologie als Geschichte* (Zürich/Stuttgart, 1967); M. Buss, "Der Sinn der Geschichte", *op. cit.*, pp. 171–96.

[11] There is a good exposé and an extensive bibliography in H. P. M. Goddijn and others, *Terzake*. Gesprekken van sociologen en theologen over kerkvernieuwing (=Kerk buiten de Kerk 4) (Utrecht, 1969).

It is true that religions themselves, particularly the so-called primitive and unknown ones, appeal to the sociologist as an object of study[12] but the time does not seem to be ripe as yet for a definite sociology of theology.

In universities such as Harvard and Yale, where from the scientific point of view there was no room for theology, sociology of religion has led to some place for a theology which would be less ideological than the theologies of before the Second World War. Here students are not afraid of starting from sociology in order to discover the starting-point of philosophical or theological systems.

Where theology takes hope as its starting-point, fully aware that one could also choose despair for this, as, for instance, in a Calvinistic theology of predestination, it is natural to ask the question whether it is really so evident that hope is a principle, i.e., that one cannot get beyond it.

In sociology one can ask whether there are no sociological "laws" that could explain the fact that a whole set of theologies opts for hope as a principle. In that case hope would not be a principle in Bloch's sense but a starting-point that is sociologically conditioned and can therefore be further explained by this sociological conditioning.[13]

This would not yet be an argument against the validity of hope as a principle of theological activity as such but it would put a brake on the premature waving of the banner of hope as a principle beyond which one cannot go. By the same token, this would make such a theology of hope more realistic.

Although so far we do not yet have a definite sociology of theology, we do have an abundant literature about a sociology of science. And if theology wants to remain a science, it must, as a science, be subjected to the criticism of this sociology of science.[14]

[12] N. Greinacher, "Wissenssoziologie und Religion", in *Internationale Dialog Zeitschr.*, 2, 2 (1969), pp. 97–101; P. L. Berger and T. Luckmann, *The Social Construction of Reality* (New York, 1966); P. L. Berger, *The Sacred Canopy*. Elements of a Sociological Theory of Religion (New York, 1967); J. Matthes, *Die Emigration der Kirche aus der Gessellschaft* (Hamburg, 1964).

[13] W. Kasper, *Die Methoden der Dogmatik*. Einheit und *Vielheit* (1967), pp. 71 and 68; J. B. Metz, *Zur Theologie der Welt* (1968); C. Dumont, "De trois dimensions retrouvées en théologie: eschatologie, orthopraxie, herméneutique", in *Nouv. Rev. Théol.*, 102, 6 (June–July, 1970), p. 583.

[14] W. Bergmann, "Zur wissenssoziologischen Analyse kirchlicher

The sociology of science is a branch of sociology as such. It examines the connection between images of reality and the actual social structures and processes. Such a sociological investigation will not query the validity of the images used by science or the ideas with which knowledge structures the reality, although the first impressions of such an investigation may rightly arouse suspicions.[15]

At present this kind of sociology is aware of the fact that scientific starting-points are co-determined by sociological conditions and of the fact that scientific approaches and ideas have an effect on social life.

It is a basic assumption of this sociology that, in both their origin and their development, ideas are influenced by social patterns of life and therefore change when society changes. On the other hand, ideas have their influence on changes in society. This precludes the notion that the world is only governed by ideas.[16] It is not by accident that the culminating points of cultures and religions occur almost exclusively in an urban society.[17]

If, then, a theologian wants to do justice to his assertion that hope is the hinge on which his theological system hangs, the principle beyond which it is impossible to go, he must remain constantly aware of what the sociology of science says about such a starting-point, namely that it is both socially determined and socially determining.[18] This does not devalue hope; it merely makes hope a relative principle instead of an absolute one.

### III. THE SCIENCE OF HISTORY

It is curious that Bloch loves to illustrate his principle of hope

---

Phänomene", in *Internationale Dialog Zeitschr.*, 2, 2 (1969), pp. 156–62; T. Luckmann, *Invisible Religion* (New York, 1967); L. Schneider (ed.), *Religion, Culture and Society* (New York, 1964), pp. 164 and 273.

[15] K. Mannheim, *Wissenssoziologie* (Berlin, 1964), pp. 309 f.

[16] C. Geertz, "Religion as a Cultural System", in *The Religious Situation*, ed. by R. Cutler (Boston, 1968); G. Gurvitch, *Vocation actuelle de la Sociologie* (2nd edn., Paris, 1957), I, p. 441; R. Bastide (ed.), *Sens et usages du terme Structure dans les sciences humaines et sociales* (The Hague, 1962); nn. 73 and 74 of the *Rev. Intern. de Phil.*, 19, pp. 249–441.

[17] A. Rüstow, *Ortsbestimmung der Gegenwart* (Zürich, 1950), p. 262.

[18] T. F. O'Dea, "Sociological dilemmas: five paradoxes of

with the phenomenon of "success": works of art that have been "successful", music that is "successful", films that are "successful", etc.[19] The modern science of history points out that history is one-sided and attributes this to the fact that historians have been inclined to chronicle only such enterprises as have been successful. In actual fact, in his effort to make history man has more often failed than succeeded. These failures should not be concealed.

Metz made the point that church history is silent about many failures and thereby wrongs both itself and Christianity at large; this is how tasks that ought to have been fulfilled have come to be forgotten and may still be forgotten; it also threatens to narrow Christianity down to only those Christian achievements that history has declared possible.[20]

If it is the purpose of written history to keep the memory alive it is also its duty always to point out the failures as well so that Christianity will continue to work at those tasks that appeared impossible at a first or second attempt.

For the modern historian the happy ending of the historical process is far from a foregone conclusion, and so man is not justified to plunge headlong and blindly into the historical process as if this were justification enough.

Bloch does not deny this basic ambiguity of history. He is fully alive to the fact that the ultimate end of history may be either "all" or "nothing". He opts for the "all" but knows that there is no final and decisive argument for this option.

Institutionalisation", in E. A. Tyriakan (ed.), *Sociological Theory. Values and sociological change* (Glencoe, 1963), pp. 71–91.

[19] See B.3 of *Das Prinzip Hoffnung* (Frankfurt, 1968), the subtitle of which is "Wunschbilder des erfüllten Augenblicke"; see also his essay, "Ueber bildende Kunst im Maschinenzeitalter", in *Literarische Augsätze* (Frankfurt, 1965), pp. 568–74.

[20] J. Mouroux, *Le mystère du temps* (Paris, 1962), p. 162; J. Girardi, *Amour chrétien et violence révolutionnaire* (Paris, 1970); S. Sandmel, *The first Christian century in Judaism and Christianity. Certainties and Uncertainties* (New York, 1969); K. Flick and Z. Alszeghy, "Teologia della Storia", in *Gregorianum*, 35 (1954), pp. 256–98; E. Castelli, *I presuppositi di una teologia della historia* (Milan, 1952); I. Berten, *Histoire, révélation et foi* (Brussels, 1969); J. B. Metz, *Weltverständnis im Glauben* (2nd edn., Mainz, 1966); W. Kasper, "Geschichtstheologie", in *Sacramentum Mundi* (Freiburg i. Br., 1967–69), cf. the register in vol. IV, s.v. "Geschichte".

In the achievement of works of art, in what he calls "the antici-
pating dream", in the harmony of music, in emotional "hunches"
about the future, and in matter, at first so recalcitrant, then yielding to the urge of human hope and desire—in all this Bloch sees
signs that this initially futile straining of human hope will find
fulfilment in human effort. The riddle contained in the alpha of
the dark beginnings will be solved in the omega of achievement
which will thus fulfil man's hope. It is not for nothing that Bloch
has been called the Teilhard de Chardin of Marxism, proclaiming a "kingdom", though not "of God".

According to Bloch we are as yet only in a preliminary stage
of history, yet so much has already been achieved in the direction
of a full and adult history that hope is no longer merely utopian
but has become a guiding principle for a mankind that must fulfil
itself in history.

Such a conception is no doubt attractive and even tempting.
But it will still have to answer the question put by the sociology
of science: Does this vision take into account the whole of reality,
including the failures that are no less historical facts than the
successes? Sometimes Bloch's argument looks too much like a
one-sided rational anticipation of the possibility of the future.

In the Christian view of history the end of history is necessarily
shrouded in darkness because for the Christian this end lies in
the hands of God and its mystery is beyond the reach of human
science. God, however, is himself the end of history in the sense
that he is also its fulfilment because he accepts and confirms it
in its unalloyed totality. This means that we should look at the
end of history not only from above in the sense of a one-sided
theology of the incarnation, but also from below, i.e., in a development within time.

History can only reach its fulfilment by the way of the cross,
*per viam crucis*, and this fulfilment is a paschal mystery, a self-
transcending made possible by grace. This willing exodus from
history towards God, however, is not a negation of history but
itself again the fulfilment of man's historical attempt to transcend
himself. In this context hope means a courageous walking into
constantly new territory with the risk of failure but with the
guarantee of a belief in God's faithfulness. This hope, made up
of historical awareness and trust in God, is very different from a

fanatical revolutionary messianism and a naïve optimism about progress.

## IV. Sects

When hope becomes too much a rational anticipation of the future it runs the risk of identifying this future too readily with what we want it to be. How far a hope, possibly guaranteed by the kergyma, can be identified with what we desire is a very debatable question. By its very nature the Christian kerygma distinguishes between what exists and what we want, and does not let us take what we want as the ultimate reality. The escape into an invisible Church in order to be able to get rid of the imperfections of the visible Church is indeed an escape. The kerygma takes shape in the concrete reality: this people of Israel, this man Jesus, this wooden cross, this concrete chaos of ecclesial communities. A hope that is blind to this concrete situation which contains elements of despair, leads to sectarianism.

In this context the increase in the number of sects[21] might well indicate a camouflaged despair which, under the mask of hope and by deliberately narrowing the perspective, tries to present the image of a successful Christianity.

Hope presupposes solidarity with all men. The individual who is called and "has succeeded" always stands for the whole of humanity, in vicariousness and solidarity, because, in goodness and evil, mankind always stands before God as one whole. When this solidarity with all men is abandoned and the *élite* principle is introduced, it becomes easier to achieve what is wanted. But in actual fact hope for all is then given up and the future is reserved

---

[21] W. J. Hollenweger, *Enthusiastisches Christentum*. Die Pfingstbewegung in Geschichte und Gegenwart (Zürich, 1969). Pages 517–75 contain a sociological and theological assessment of the Pentecostal movement (which the author does range with the sects) where it is pointed out that this movement appeals to those who, materially, economically or in some other way, live "on the dark side of life"; see also "Südkoreas Entwicklungskrise: Christentum im Schatten 'neuer Religionen' ", in *Herder Korrespondenz* (1969), 11, pp. 517–8; "Man for all sects", in *Time*, 55 (17 Oct. 1969); E. Fulling, "Neue Religion in Brasilien heute", in *Lutherische Monatshefte*, 12 (Dec. 1969), pp. 616–20; V. H. Hine, "Pentecostal Glossolalia: Toward a functional Interpretation", in *Journal for the Scient. Study of Religion*, 2 (1969), pp. 211–26.

for a small group. What seems incapable of universal achievement because of an anthropological gravity created by the universal burden of all men might succeed in a small group.

In reality this is a gesture of despair because by creating a sect one admits that one does not believe in salvation for all. One may try to legitimize this procedure ideologically by appealing, out of context, to the small remnant or the small flock of Scripture, but in fact one shows despair of universal salvation. The history of the sects shows that they start among men who despair of Christianity as it exists and try to find a confirmation of their *élite* ideology in pietistic experiences. In this sense, therefore, the increase in the number of sects within Christianity is a sign of camouflaged despair. This is why the sect usually recruits its adepts among the underdogs, that lower level of society which lacks identification and receives no sign of acceptance from this society.

A recent study of Kitzinger's[22] on the Rastafari sect in Jamaica not only confirms this view but shows that the perspective has become so narrow that even within the sect there is only salvation for man, while woman only moves on the periphery. The object of hope is not only narrowed down and anticipated by making the wish to return to Africa the keynote but also by reserving the future to men only. This last point could well be an exaggeration of a tendency which one can observe at a more acceptable level within Christianity as soon as there is talk of making room for woman in the official functions of the Church.

One may also wonder here whether drug-users[23] are not victims of some similar frustration of hope. It seems to be characteristic of these drug-users that they may become integrated again into society *via* one or other sect. In that case the sequence: drug-user, member of a sect, integrated member of society, might reveal a gradual broadening of the perspective, apart from the therapeutic effect. But this suggests a value-judgment that should first be verified by further study.

[22] S. Kitzinger, "Protest and Mysticism: the Rastafari Cult of Jamaica", in *Journal for Sc. St. of Rel.*, 2 (1969), pp. 240–62).
[23] T. Robbins, "Eastern Mysticism and the resocialization of drug users", in *Journal for Sc. St. of Rel.*, 2 (1969), pp. 240–62; see also Salman's art. in the 1969 issue of *Concilium on Spirituality* (American edn., vol. 49).

A trend similar to that prevailing at the formation of a sect can be traced at another level in movements like that of the hippies. We do not mean, of course, to characterize the whole of hippidom in this way. But the symbolism of a paradise-situation created by pulling out of the chaos is there. This symbolism is even present in the problem implied in the "generation-gap": the claim of groups of young people and student revolutions has something of this "writing-off" of the older generation where salvation is concerned.[24] Basically this, too, is an expression of an *élite* mentality of despair with regard to the older generation, accompanied by a narrowed-down pattern of hope for the young.

Movements like the hippies seem to rest on this ideology of "hope for the *élite*", and this precludes the universality of what one desires for the future. The hippies have occasionally been described as "the Freudian proletariat".[25] The reason for this may be that they think they can appeal to Freud[26] as the originator of a theory that life must be lived to the full: what one can expect of life is the free rein given to the primary urges. This appeal to Freud can hardly be justified. Leary advised the hippies to "turn on, tune in and drop out; do your own thing". This does not satisfy the top layer of hippidom, where this kind of advice is seen as a recipe for extreme individualism.

## V. Isolation

A new form of isolation and alienation[27] seems to be closely connected with what has just been said. This isolation first of all affects people who, as it is put euphemistically, have reached the terminal phase. This refers to people who are of no use to the productive society because they can no longer produce and people

[24] L. Yablonski, *The Hippie Trip* (New York, 1968); cf. N. Beets, "Drugs: op zoek naar het beloofde land", in *Dux* (June, 1970), pp. 313–20; M. Cornaton, "Perspectives et limites de la psychosociologie", in *Etudes* (April 1969), pp. 540–53.

[25] J. van Ussel, "Oude en nieuwe mythen", in *Dux* (May 1970), pp. 245–55; cf. *ibid.*, p. 258; J. D. Brown (ed.), *The Hippies* (New York, 1966).

[26] P. Ricoeur, *De l'interprétation* (Paris, 1968), pp. 154–85; L. Beirnaert, "Introduction à la psychoanalyse freudienne de la religion", in *Etudes* (Feb. 1968), pp. 200–10.

[27] H. P. Dreitzel, "Einsamkeit als soziologisches Problem", in *Wissenschaft und Praxis*, 59, 3 (March 1970), pp. 102–20.

given up by medical science with whom society no longer communicates in a way significant enough to give meaning to their lives.[28] Both these forms of the terminal phase lead rather to despair than to hope. In fact, some have described this terminal phase as an anticipated death.[29]

One might see this isolation as a fringe phenomenon that does not attack the whole of society, although it still ought to make us more critically alert when we talk of hope in theology.

There is, however, a form of isolation, which Gadamer[30] has drawn attention to, and which affects the whole of society more profoundly, namely, the rift between human activity and a technological society.[31] Marx already pointed out that a capitalist society alienates man from his labour. This particular alienation concerns all classes and not only the workers: people no longer see any sense in what they are doing, and this shows itself already, like a new form of quietism, in the unwillingness to work among young people. Given that man not only plays a part in this technological society[32] but actually *is* his labour, then it becomes clear that we have here a curious kind of collective alienation which will make it increasingly harder for man to achieve an identification at the same level as that reached by the growth of his historical consciousness.[33] It is not without good reason that David Riesman[34] gave his book the significant title of "The Lonely Crowd", because man's personal creativity is being frustrated by the fact that his tasks are merely dictated by the technical condition that rules the masses and man is reduced to a mere executive of whatever this anonymous society has planned for him. This takes all privacy out of whatever he has to do and stigmatizes all

[28] E. Goffman, *Stigma*. Notes on the management of spoiled identity (New York, 1963).

[29] S. de Beauvoir, *La vieillesse* (Paris, 1970), pp. 230–99: "La vieillesse dans la société d'aujourd'hui".

[30] H. G. Gadamer, "Vereinsamung als Symptom von Selbstentfremdung", in *Wissenschaft und Praxis*, 59, 3 (March 1970), pp. 85–93.

[31] *Loc. cit.*, p. 89; Y. Spiegel, *Theologie der bürgerlichen Gesellschaft* (Munich, 1968).

[32] H. P. Dreitzel, *Die gesellschaftlichen Leiden und das Leiden an der Gesellschaft* (Stuttgart, 1968).

[33] P. A. Baran, *Das Engagement des Intellektuellen* (Rotbach, 1961), p. 16.

[34] D. Riesman, *Die Einsame Masse*. Eine Untersuchung über die Wandlungen des amerikanischen Characters (Hamburg, 1958).

attempts at creating a human personality.[35] The fact that this society will in the future necessarily become still more technical-minded will hardly lead to hope but rather to despair since it is no longer possible to discover the human meaning of such a society.

## SUICIDE

Every day 1,000 people die by suicide, and one may take it that every day 10,000 people attempt suicide but fail for one reason or another.[36] The United States has 17,000 suicides per annum. The increase in numbers bears no relation to the increase in world-population. Categories of people among whom suicide used to be the exception now show a disturbingly high percentage. According to the World Health Organization suicide is one of the ten principal causes of death in industrial countries. According to E. Ringel[37] it has become a world problem.

One of the many works written about suicide is called *The End of Hope*, but there is as yet no monograph on the relation between despair and suicide although this is one of the dominant motives.[38] This present documentation cannot go into detail about this point, but we wish to point to this rise in the number of suicides as an indication of despair because this factual situation is relevant to any theological treatment of hope.

On the other hand, a positive relationship has been established between unbelief and suicide. Practically all researchers[39] are of the opinion that there is a connection between suicide and absence of religion ("irreligiosity"). Masrijk[40] even thinks that the inclination to suicide is ultimately always caused by unbelief.

[35] E. Goffman, *Stigma, loc. cit.*, p. 47.
[36] N. Speijer, *Het zelfmoordvraagstuk* (Arnhem, 1969), p. 8.
[37] E. Ringel, "La prévention du suicide. Un problème mondial", in *Hygiène mentale* (1968), p. 84.
[38] J. A. M. Meerloo, *Suicide and Mass-suicide* (New York, 1962), p. 26. This author is the only one who has methodically worked out a more or less complete scheme of the conscious and unconscious causes of suicide.
[39] J. A. Morphew, "Religion and attempted suicide", in *Intern. Journal Soc. Psych.*, 14 (1968), p. 188; M. Bertin, "Etude statistique du suicide", in *Cahiers Laënnec* (1966), p. 5; cf. Shneidmann's bibliography in his *The Cry for Help* (1961), which contains over 3,900 items.
[40] *Der Selbstmord als soziale Massenerscheinung der modernen Civilisation* (Vienna, 1881); J. D. Douglas, *The Social Meaning of Suicide* (Princeton, 1967).

Durkheim, who did pioneer work in this field in order to rid suicide of a moralistic taboo by means of a sociological approach to the problem,[41] had already discovered that there is an inverse ratio between the number of suicides and the degree of integration in the social group to which the individual belonged. All cases that have been studied can apparently be attributed to social disintegration and disinstitutionalization. This is fostered by the systematic relegation of death from society and the refusal to think about death. This world-problem is one of the most distressing manifestations of despair with which modern society is saddled.[42]

## VII. BEING ABANDONED BY GOD

The eclipse of God, which has both a theoretical negative aspect and a positive ethical one,[43] can be one of the factors that take away hope. Bloch[44] has spoken of the "gracefulness" of the future by which he means that what lies in front of man is not only enigmatic and faceless but also shows a certain benevolence and a willingness to co-operate.

Christian hope puts this in more personal terms: God who is not only the past and the present but also the future has a face and comes to meet man: He is the one who is coming.[45] This "future" is not only something to work out, but to live with and

[41] *Le Suicide*, of 1897, is the first real scientific sociological study about suicide and still influences the sociological study of this problem.

[42] A. Mathé, "Les suicides des vieillards", in *Vie Médic.*, 91 (1967), p. 48; J. J. Kockelmans, "On suicide: Reflexions upon Camus' view of the problem", in *The Psychoanalytic Rev.*, 54 (1967), p. 441; P. L. Landsberg, *Essai sur l'expérience de la mort suivi du problème moral du suicide* (Paris, 1961).

[43] The theoretical negative aspect runs through the whole literature about the "God is dead" theology; the positive ethical aspect emerges in the Christian "night-of-the-soul" mysticism, and is called purification—cf. J. Peters, *De volledige werken van Sint Jan van het Kruis, ingeleid en vertaald* (Hilversum, 1963), pp. 54-8, 145-84, 817-954; P. Lucien, *L'Expérience de Dieu* (Paris, 1968).

[44] I. Fetscher and W. Strolz, *Ernst Bloch—Wegzeichen der Hoffnung* (Freiburg i. Br., 1967), p. 17: "Gunst der Realität; das Objekt ist kooperierendes Subjekt".

[45] H. G. Cox, *On not leaving it to the Snake* (1968), p. 12; E. Schillebeeckx, "Het 'rechte' geloof", etc., *loc. cit.*, pp. 135-7; J. Leclerq, *L'Amour des lettres et le désir de Dieu* (Paris/Bruges, 1957).

to have a dialogue with as if it were a person. When the future is experienced as a void and ultimately without meaning, it creates anxiety. When it begins to show the signs and features of the God of the promises, it brings hope.

Atheists, and especially the kind of people who have a blind faith in progress, see in Christian hope an obstacle to progress in the sense that Christian providence must be replaced by scientific progress.[46] By this criticism they want to attack a kind of hope that shifts the responsibility for the future on to a God beyond time where the final conclusion of history has already been fixed from all eternity. But God's eternity does not primarily mean timelessness in the Greek sense, but a more positive being above time, free to found history and to enter into this history without being overwhelmed by it but rather infusing newness into it in a decisive way.

Both on the part of God and of man it is the decision that constantly creates the future. This mutual decision in a freedom which man must constantly acquire anew, also makes the Covenant something that is constantly new and not something concluded for ever in the past. It is the experience of decision that turns hope into a category of experience which can overcome anxiety and despair.

But this implies that one can only speak of hope if one also speaks of despair. We cannot abolish the dialectic between hope and despair with impunity. For in that case hope would lose its dynamic character and degenerate into a quietistic ideology which deprives hope of its Christian depth and the Christian of that spiritual sanity which is part of salvation. To the question whether there is certainty in this dialectic hope one can only answer as K. Barth did when asked: "Is there certainty of faith, Professor?" He replied: "Nothing gives certainty of faith: *He* gives it."[47]

---

[46] W. Kasper, *loc. cit.*, p. 280.
[47] Quoted by C. J. Dippel, "Tolk en getuige in een tijd zonder herinnering en zonder verwachting", in *Wending* (June 1970), p. 228.

*Translated by Theo Westow*

the keys to re. newal

Offenses against our fellow men bring personal feelings of guilt and despair. What, then, is the way to restoration of peace and hope? Alvin Rogness points to the way in **FORGIVENESS & CONFESSION.** **$1.50**

Dorothee Sölle proposes something **BEYOND MERE OBEDIENCE.** Something above blind faith. Our God-given freedom should be released to imagine and create rewarding lives, as manifested in the life style of Jesus. **$2.25**

**MODERN SCIENCE AND CHRISTIAN LIFE** Do science and theology actually conflict? Stanley Beck explores various theories and offers some revealing explanation of these two varying realms of human understanding. **$2.95**

**THE BEGINNING OF THE CHURCH IN THE NEW TESTAMENT** by Ferdinand Hahn, August Strobel, Eduard Schweizer. Three New Testament scholars explore the beginnings of the church to discover patterns for today's disciples. Nov. 2 **$2.25**

**PERSONAL FAITH FOR HUMAN CRISES** Today's "knowledge explosion" creates crises never before imagined. Louis Accola points to creative, meaningful responses to these crises. Oct. 5 **$2.75**

John Halvorson characterizes B.C. and A.D. as **THE AGES IN TENSION.** What opportunities exist for Christians who live in the New age of grace? How does the Old age influence the New? **$1.95**

**LUTHERANS IN BRAZIL** How did the Lutheran church come to emerge in Brazil? E. Theodore Bachman traces the struggle from its beginnings to today's growing, active Lutheran communion. **$2.00**

How can a minister best continue his education? Editor James Hofrenning in **THE CONTINUING QUEST** suggests guides for furthering his personal growth in the ministry. Nov. 2 **$4.95**

## AT YOUR BOOKSTORE

**ugsburg** PUBLISHING HOUSE   MINNEAPOLIS, MINNESOTA 55415